Central American Refugees
and U.S. High Schools

Central American Refugees and U.S. High Schools

A Psychosocial Study of
Motivation and Achievement

MARCELO M. SUAREZ-OROZCO

STANFORD UNIVERSITY PRESS   1989
STANFORD, CALIFORNIA

Stanford University Press
Stanford, California
© 1989 by the Board of Trustees
of the Leland Stanford Junior University
Printed in the United States of America

Published with the assistance of the
Andrew W. Mellon Foundation

CIP data are at the end of the book

For Fingal Aquiles Suárez Orozco,
Maria Nydia L. de Suárez Orozco,
and Carola

Preface

THIS BOOK, quite unintentionally, captures the human side of the headlines that dominated public attention in the United States during much of the 1980's. Central America has captured and polarized the American public mind like no other region of the world since Vietnam. In mid-1987, the nation was hypnotized by the congressional hearings investigating the ostensibly illegal diversion of funds from secret weapons sales to Iran to the Contra forces fighting the Sandinistas in Nicaragua. The highly controversial decision to divert the profits underscored the almost monomaniacal dedication with which Washington came to pursue its objectives in Central America.

It is hard to establish just how a collection of such small nations in Central America had entered the mainstream of the public discourse on U.S. foreign policy. Whether what is unfolding in Central America is, on the one hand, a new phase of an old and dangerous East-West contest for the minds and souls of a Third World people, or, on the other hand, the challenging by a poor people of an old order of inequality historically administered in Washington as much as in Managua or San Salvador or Guatemala City is likely to be passionately debated by scholars, politicians, and the press for years to come. Yet, regardless of the argument, the kinds of issues derivative of these grand historical and ideological questions will inevitably include the lives of thinking and feeling human beings who find themselves, quite literally, caught between forces basically foreign to their hearts.

This essay is a psychosocial study of the experience of a group of Central American youths recently arrived in the United States.

Driven to escape the wars and deprivations in their native Central America, such youths have been entering the United States by the tens of thousands within the past decade. In the following pages, I explore their hopes, fears, dreams, and deeds in the new land. In the process of resettling in an affluent society, the youngsters came to share the dream of older generations of immigrants to the United States: to establish for themselves a position that would enable them to help loved ones still living and struggling in the old country. In pursuing that dream, they came to endure great sacrifices, in the almost unshakable conviction that short-term hardships would in the long run bring them and their loved ones the benefits of a better life. In so resolutely accepting the sacrifices and hardships, these youths evince a psychosocial motivational pattern of considerable theoretical interest. The goal of this book is to analyze the significance of that pattern, and pursuing that goal will, of necessity, lead us to the heart of current thinking on the nature of human motivational dynamics. Accordingly, a parallel objective of the book is to develop a psychosocial critique of motivation theory as framed in the psychological, sociological, and anthropological literatures.

I must say a word about the intellectual kinship of the research I report in this forum. In my view, this work lies in the culture-and-personality tradition in American anthropology first articulated in the writings of Franz Boas's students (Ruth Benedict, Margaret Mead, and Edward Sapir) and their colleagues (Gregory Bateson, Cora Du Bois, Abram Kardiner, and Ralph Linton), and in the works of their intellectual heirs, the elders of what we now call psychological anthropology: Victor Barnouw, George A. De Vos, Alfred I. Hallowell, Francis Hsu, Weston La Barre, Robert Le Vine, George Spindler, Melford Spiro, John Whiting, and others. These scholars, disparate though they are both in area of expertise and in theoretical bias, share the vision that human psychology must be approached from a dual perspective, exploring both social-structural variables and personality variables within a distinct cultural heritage. Throughout the book, whether considering the substratum of encounters with the culture of terror in Central America or the emergent juxtaposition of achievement themes with a wish to nurture relatives left behind, I shall situate the lives and behavior of these people both in personality-motivational dynamics and in the changing social milieu that envelops the experiential self.

The book originated as a doctoral dissertation on minority status schooling problems in a plural society. It was in a preliminary research project on the social context of learning in bilingual classrooms that I first came across a small group of new arrivals from Central America. The focus of that research was the Mexican-American experience in the American classroom, but it soon became clear to me that although the new arrivals from Central America shared with their Mexican-American classmates a knowledge of Spanish, their psychosocial concerns and particular educational problems were quite different. Although I had been in Central America in 1974 with Dr. Horacio Erausquin and his sons Rod and Gonny Erausquin, as part of a vaguely medical excursion that took us by car from San Francisco, California, to Buenos Aires, Argentina, I had heretofore been ignorant of the Central American experience in the United States. The questions raised by these youngsters required another research project, one concentrating more specifically on the Central American case. Thus a new research project was conceived.

The book concludes six years of apprenticeship in the Department of Anthropology at the University of California, Berkeley. I remain deeply thankful to the anthropology faculty as a whole for making my journey through Kroeber Hall intellectually daring as well as personally gratifying. A Robert H. Lowie Graduate Scholarship and a University of California Regents Fellowship made this study possible.

Among the Berkeley faculty, I had the privilege of working closely with a number of scholars whose brilliance and sense of dedication to the field is matched only by their personal sensitivity and kindness. Professor George De Vos directed this study and has otherwise influenced my thinking in more ways than I can fully recognize. I believe he knows that I know what he has done for me over the years, since a rainy fall day nine years ago when I first entered his office to inquire about his field, psychological anthropology. Since then he has been an immense source of inspiration and guidance. Additionally, Suzanne Lake De Vos kindly read the entire manuscript and offered many helpful suggestions.

Professor John U. Ogbu helped formulate many of the questions that motivated the research reported in this book. Professor Ogbu's intellectual force and uncompromising sense of scholarly integrity when facing difficult and sensitive questions have been examples as I begin to face some of the same issues in my own work. Professor Stanley H. Brandes guided me during the most difficult phases of my training at Berkeley: he was my first adviser in anthropology and I was his teaching assistant when my father died in mid-1985. Professor Brandes's creativity, sensitivity, and scholarly production have made him most popular among students at Berkeley.

Professor Alan Dundes has been a major influence in my academic training. Professor Dundes's brilliance and monumental bibliographic knowledge have forever affected my relationship with the printed word. He teaches not only how to formulate critical questions, but also how to introduce such questions into formal scholarly discourse.

Two other scholars have affected my intellectual development. Professor Donald Hansen, of the Graduate School of Education at Berkeley, and Dr. Victoria Johnson, of Stanford University, introduced me to ethnographic fieldwork as a research assistant in their project on the Social Context of Learning in Bilingual Classrooms. They taught me many things, including the skills of fieldwork I have now made my own.

I have had the privilege of presenting many of the thoughts contained in this book in lectures around the country. I wish to thank audiences, particularly students, at the University of California, Berkeley; University of California, Los Angeles; University of California, Santa Barbara; University of California, Santa Cruz; University of California, San Diego; the University of Chicago; the University of Wisconsin-Madison; the University of Pennsylvania; Princeton University; and Stanford University. They showed themselves to be relentless in formulating challenging questions. As most teachers know, our real education begins when we face students in the classrooms. And, even in the age when the American university has come under attack for contributing to our social malaise, I have found my own students to be a source of fresh inspiration. To them goes my admiration for their uncompromising academic skepticism in an age of prefabricated intellectual consumerism.

William W. Carver, editor at Stanford University Press, guided this project from the outset with dedication and professionalism. His perceptive queries led me to see where my own thoughts or data and the printed page did not quite match.

Carola and Marisa, my wife and daughter, have, in a very real and immediate way, made this book possible. Carola selflessly gave of herself to help me complete the research presented here. She patiently but critically listened to my emerging ideas from the very first day of work in the field to the final draft of the manuscript. Throughout, Carola's love and patience made the work in the field and the writing that much more gratifying. Marisa, who broke my heart every time she would come looking for me to paint with her, only to close the door to my office when she saw me in front of my computer transcribing field notes or working on a section of a chapter, saying, as if trying to alleviate her sense of disappointment, "Daddy is working," has brought into my life the kind of happiness only poets can put into words.

I remain thankful to the school district where part of the research reported here was conducted. For obvious reasons of confidentiality, I cannot name individuals. I do wish to thank specifically the principals of both "Joaquin" and "Jefferson" high schools for opening their doors to me, knowing full well, I think, that I would not find a rose garden in their conflict-ridden inner-city schools. I also wish to thank the teachers who allowed me into their classrooms and who made my journey through the schools as enjoyable as it could be.

Finally, I wish to thank my informants, the youths with the dream. Again, confidentiality prevents me from naming the individuals who took me into their lives and entrusted to me their dreams, fears, joys, and sorrows. They taught me an unforgettable lesson on the human will to love. *Muchas gracias y buena suerte.*

M.S.-O.

Contents

A map of Central America is on p. 74

Figures and Tables

Figures

Tables

Abbreviations

The following abbreviations are used in the text.

CRECEN Central American Refugee Committee

HPDP Hispanic Policy Development Project

SYB Statistical Yearbook of the Immigration and Naturalization Service

USDS United States Department of State

Central American Refugees
and U.S. High Schools

ONE

Introduction

THE OBJECTIVE of this book is to document and interpret
certain key issues in the lives and experiences of a sampling
of recent immigrants to the United States from the war-torn
Central American nations.* In the fall of 1984, armed with notebooks, a tape recorder, a native command of the Spanish language, and the standard "anthropological right to be ignorant"
about the people under consideration (Colson 1974: xv), I began
a year-long ethnographic study among new immigrants, to learn
about their dreams, their deeds, and their lives. Moreover, there
was the larger research context of minority status and schooling
issues in a pluralistic society. How were they adapting to change?
What problems did they confront in the new land? How did
their experiences in their countries affect the way they faced life
in the United States? How were the youngsters adapting to
American schooling? Did they follow a pattern similar to that of
other, better-known ethnic groups? What issues were the new
arrivals encountering in an American educational system that
was increasingly coming under fire as ineffective or worse? (See
Hansen and Johnson 1985; Gardner 1983.)

In order to explore these and other issues, I spent a year
among Central American immigrants in a major urban center in
the western United States, concentrating on issues regarding
schooling, work, and family life. As the research progressed, I
gained entrance to two schools, each with about 600 recent immigrants from Spanish-speaking countries: mostly El Salvador,

---

* I use the term *immigrant* to refer to those who come into a new country, region, or environment in order to settle there, more or less permanently.

Guatemala, and Nicaragua.* These schools provided classes in English as a Second Language (ESL) and bilingual classes in mathematics, history, U.S. government, and some other subjects. Newcomers were first tested at the district's "Intake Center" to determine grade level and language proficiency. Students judged to have "no English proficiency" or "limited English proficiency" were routed to these two schools, which we shall call Joaquin High School and Jefferson High School.

Both schools were in the inner city. The student body of each was over 90 percent minority. Joaquin High had a student population that was about 33 percent Spanish-speaking;† about 20 percent were Chinese, with a sprinkling of other Asians; about 14 percent were Black, and 12 percent Filipino. Only about 5 percent of the students were classified as "other White," and the remaining 16 percent were "other non-White." In Jefferson High 25 percent of the students were Spanish-speaking, 30 percent were Black, 20 percent were Filipino, and about 13 percent were Chinese or other Asian. Only 3 percent were classified as "other White" and 9 percent as "other non-White." At both schools, close to 50 percent of the students were immigrants, from either Latin America or Asia.

During my year of research at these institutions, the mobility rate was extremely high. For example, in June 1984 Jefferson High enrolled about 1,500 students, but during the school year some 900 new students enrolled in the school and 918 were dropped from the school rolls. At Joaquin High the initial student enrollment in June 1984 was about 1,900 students, but by late January 1985 there were 680 new students and 600 others had been dropped from the rolls.

Joaquin High is located in a particularly decayed neighborhood in the inner city. Prostitutes sold their services within a three-block radius of the school, and pushers regularly peddled their drugs all around the school. In fact, marijuana, hashish, cocaine (including "crack"), barbiturates, "speed," and the like were all readily available, even in the school yard. "Street people," some

---

* Among the 600, there were also students from Mexico and South America, mostly Colombia, Venezuela, and Peru. I do not consider their experiences in the present work.

† This figure includes new arrivals from Central America, U.S.-born Hispanics, and immigrants from Mexico and South America.

with obvious psychotic problems, could be found wandering aimlessly in the vicinity. Jefferson High sits within an industrial area, among factories and canneries. Though there were then no prostitutes in its immediate precincts, illicit drugs were abundant and openly trafficked.

Walking toward the principal's office on my first day at Jefferson High, I observed three Black youths smoking marijuana a few yards from the front gate. As I passed by, they continued their activity as if I were invisible. I felt like intervening, but since it was my first day there, I thought I should not begin my work in an adversary role with the students. Eventually I learned that my behavior was not unexpected. They already knew what I soon learned: that many teachers dealt with such situations by simply ignoring them, in order to avoid conflict.

Both schools had bad reputations in the city for gang violence. One afternoon, shortly before Christmas vacation, a group of Black youths, armed with baseball bats and golf clubs, assaulted a group of Vietnamese students in the middle of the school yard. When the affair was over a few minutes later, an ambulance took three youths to the city hospital for treatment. The episode was allegedly in retaliation for a prior encounter in which two Vietnamese students had beaten up a Black youth. In fact, none of the victims of the assault had participated in the initial encounter, and the retaliation was at random, a form of ethnic "collective punishment." They just happened to be Vietnamese. Even toward the end of the study, I still felt jarred by the frequent sight of city police cars, lights flashing, parked in front of the schools.

A chronic sense of fear permeated both schools. The teachers themselves were very much afraid of their students. One teacher in the regular English program confessed over lunch that he wore a tie to "impress" his students: "a suit intimidates them," he said. The new arrivals from Central America became very fearful of members of other ethnic groups. Informants routinely reported that their American peers stole their bus passes. The new arrivals, both male and female, and not only the Latin Americans, were apt to be beaten and/or robbed in the schools. In a perverse twist, the immigrants traded their old Central American terrors for new inner-city fears.

The principals in both schools were young—in their early

thirties—energetic, and seriously concerned about the issues that plagued their schools: gang violence, low performance, and a high student turnover. I met the principals separately and presented to them a vague picture of what I intended to do. I myself was not sure of what I would find, and I did not want my presence to be seen as an intervention designed to bring about change. I did not inform them of my particular interests in dropout patterns or in possible high-achievement patterns among some students. It had already been reported in the literature that immigrant students such as the Chinese were doing relatively well, whereas Blacks and Mexican American students continued to do poorly (Ogbu and Matute-Bianchi 1986: 99–130). How would new Central American immigrants respond to the American educational system?

The Ethnographer at School

In order to explore this question from an anthropological perspective, I hoped to spend time observing in the schools, getting to know the recent arrivals and their teachers, and gaining their trust. Only then would I begin to concentrate on the patterns that appeared to merit follow-up study. It was impossible to predict what conclusions might emerge.

At the outset, my lack of a settled research agenda put me in an awkward position vis-à-vis the principals and teachers. Because I was a Hispanic affiliated with a prestigious university and had already done research on issues of minority schooling, they looked to me as an expert who could provide answers and solutions to the enormous problems they faced. Yet I wanted to avoid becoming their pedagogical handyman, for fear the study would suffer, and I was not sure that my research would result in any easily applied recommendations. I was concerned first with answering basic research questions that would, upon completion of the study, return me to the theoretical area of minority status, achievement motivation, and schooling in a pluralistic society. This posed for me a number of serious ethical and practical problems.

It would be quite proper for me to make it clear to the principals and teachers that I was there to learn, not to advise; that, even though I was familiar with the theoretical debates concerning minority status and schooling, I was investigating a specific new immigrant population that had heretofore not been considered by social scientists. Second, I noted that there were several alternative approaches to explaining the problems facing minority students in schools, but no consensus in the field. Different schools of thought emphasized different themes, such as language influences, discourse, value orientation, and social stratification. Thus, my own opinions and recommendations might be considered biased by colleagues not sharing certain assumptions.

I proposed finally what I believed to be a mutually beneficial way for the staff to make use of my skills. I offered to help teachers and counselors in their daily routines. Jefferson's principal, Mr. Washington, agreed. He thought it would be best to let each teacher use my skills as she or he deemed appropriate. Joaquin's principal, Ms. Arthur, put me in contact with the bilingual counselor, and within a few weeks I began to work each morning for two to three hours in the counseling office. My experiences there turned out to be critical to my subsequent understanding of how the schools were "tracking" new immigrant students into a course of study of dubious pedagogical value. Working with the counselors led me to conclude that their office generally attempted to deter even the most motivated and brightest students from pursuing any plans of higher education. For example, rather than concern herself with developing an integral program of study for students, the Spanish-speaking counselor placed students in classes in almost an assembly-line fashion, without regard for their individual prior record of study, current level of functioning, or aspirations for the future. As a result, a number of informants reported a sense of frustration at wasting time taking classes they had already successfully completed in Central America, two and even three years earlier. Yet the counselor would often dismiss their request for more advanced classes as irrelevant. One immigrant told me with rage in his voice, "She said algebra in my country is 'different' from American algebra!"

The work in the counseling office allowed me to explore how some students adopted successful strategies for overcoming these school-imposed barriers. In order to avoid any open confrontations with the counselors, they would approach a sympathetic faculty member for help in rectifying a given problem or injustice. When Hector, who later graduated from Joaquin and went on to a premedical program at a Midwestern university, was a junior in high school, freshly arrived from El Salvador, the counselor had assigned him to take algebra, which he had taken in his homeland. He felt that repeating the course would be a waste of time, so he approached the teacher of an advanced course in geometry with a request to take that course. The teacher was kind enough to take an interest in him and offered to test his level of functioning in the subject. After Hector passed the test, the teacher himself asked the counselor to allow Hector to change class. Hector enrolled and passed the more advanced course in geometry.

Another informant tried a similar tactic, but the counselor was adamant. To avoid the dreary prospect of repeating a subject he had already learned in a Guatemalan high school, the student arranged with a teacher to take the advanced course in geometry but to receive formal credit for the lower-level algebra class the counselor had decided he needed. These episodes reflect the unshakable determination to succeed displayed by some informants, an attitude we shall return to in Chapter 6.

Jefferson High had no bilingual counselor, yet there were about 350 Spanish-speaking students classified as "non-English speakers." Joaquin's only fully bilingual counselor, Ms. Mosco, had responsibility for 350 recent immigrants from Spanish-speaking countries, some from Mexico, some from Central America and South America. She reported being overworked, yet more than once I saw her at her desk in the middle of a work day, reading a newspaper. Ms. Mosco was a Central American herself but seemed biased against the new arrivals. A class factor may have been at work here: she was a middle-class Salvadorean who had spent more than twenty years in the United States, and she seemed to display a negative attitude toward the recent lower-class arrivals. "They are all liars," she once said when I reported that I could not get through to two parents she had requested I contact; "they give us the wrong phone number so we can't track them down." Some months later, when I was organizing a Parents' Day meeting at the school, she prophesied failure:

"They won't come," she said. "These people are not interested in their children's schooling." In the event, so many parents and guardians (over 40 in all) came to the meeting that there were not enough chairs for everyone.

Both principals, at least, were eager to participate in the study. They kept their doors open to me during the entire research period and advised their school personnel to be cooperative. Throughout the year, I was able to talk to each of them at length about their careers, the schools, and the problems they faced.

As the research progressed, I began to feel more comfortable at Joaquin High School. Although Jefferson's principal impressed me as a capable figure with a strong presence, some of his staff were defensive with respect to my research. The vice-principal, a Filipino, asked why I did not study Filipinos, and why "all the research money goes into studying Latinos." I replied that many anthropologists had studied Filipinos and that in fact we knew little about the new immigrants from Central America. Like some other school personnel, she seemed incapable of differentiating the Central American students from the larger, more amorphous "Latino" category.

Within weeks the routine that would characterize the first six months of the research was set. I spent three days of the week in one school and two in the other, alternating the 3:2 pattern to distribute my time more evenly. I attended the classes of three teachers at Joaquin High and of two teachers at Jefferson High, and later added another class at each school. I continued to spend three hours a day in Joaquin's counseling office working with students and their parents or guardians. In the classrooms, I sat in the back row and took notes, trying to be as unobtrusive as possible. Increasingly, however, both teachers and students turned to me for assistance. Would I help grade some tests? or get a film for the next period? or give a presentation to the class on what anthropologists do? The students wanted to know what I was doing. Was I a teacher? studying to be a teacher? a teachers' teacher? How do you say *tarde* in English? How do you spell "especially"? Where do we get the vaccinations required to stay in school? Would I help fill out a job application?

Soon the word was out that I was of some use. Teachers began to rely on my daily help. I had become a teachers' aide. The new immigrants began actively to search me out for help with their homework or with questions about a new job, moving to a new place, or filling out some forms. One day a group of Central American students at Jefferson High approached me: they wanted to know more about universities in the United States, about programs, costs, requirements, and so on. At that point, I realized that Jefferson's college counselor spoke no Spanish, and the students felt uneasy talking to her in their broken English. They asked me to make an informal presentation on college in the United States. I met with sixteen new immigrant seniors and juniors at lunchtime. Their questions made it clear that they were interested in learning more about postsecondary educational opportunities, but were largely ignorant of the most basic facts. A seemingly paradoxical juxtaposition of extremely high aspirations and a lack of knowledge regarding some key implementation issues surfaced repeatedly in my conversations with youngsters. They aimed high but were sometimes at a loss when it came to translating their dreams into deeds. José, a senior from Guatemala with an impressive grade point average [GPA], wanted to go on to college but was uncertain whether American universities accepted foreigners. Months later, I learned that what he really wanted to know was whether undocumented students might be accepted in college. Their concern about their residency status was notably evident when they spoke of their wishes for a college education.*

Eager for knowledge also about postsecondary educational opportunities, a group of immigrant students were making an effort to fill a vacuum that existed in the school's counseling office. Several students organized informational visits to a number of colleges and universities.

At Joaquin High the principal became aware that I was doing a great deal of work for the school and the students, helping applicants fill out forms after school, or talking to them about their experiences and plans for the future. She saw me discussing the differences between graduation requirements and college entrance requirements with concerned parents and guardians. I think she began to feel somewhat embarrassed, for I was obviously satisfying a demand for services that the paid school

---

* New arrivals did not need to produce proof of residency status in order to enroll in high school. In order to enter college, however, they had to declare their residency status formally.

staff was not providing. One morning, when she had invited me to her office, she commented that I had "become indispensable around here," and offered me a paid position as "bilingual parent/community liaison." Now I would no longer have observer status but would be paid for work that I had been doing for free.

The new responsibilities changed my schedule. I would spend the entire morning in classrooms, working with the teachers and the students. I would spend the afternoons in my new capacity, meeting parents, guardians, and relatives to discover problem areas and mediating between monolingual Spanish-speaking adults/youngsters and monolingual English-speaking teachers/staff. One vignette illustrates what my new duties involved. Doña Garcia was the guardian of her grandson, Pedro, a 15-year-old student from El Salvador. Pedro had been at home for about ten days on account of illness, and the monolingual Spanish-speaking elderly lady received a recorded telephone message each morning, in English. She could understand only something about "Joaquin High School." After the third or fourth day, she came to school to find out the meaning of the message, and she was referred to me.

I then discovered that both Joaquin and Jefferson schools used a taped, computer-operated calling system to report any absences of students from a particular household. That the recorded message was in English, and that a large proportion of the households represented in the schools spoke little or no English, had not been considered by the authorities. Eventually, Joaquin High purchased a machine that transmitted messages in several languages.

In the course of my new job, I discovered that few of the immigrant students were in the United States with all members of their nuclear family. In fact, the majority of my informants had left one or more family members behind in Central America and were living here with other relatives or with friends. It was in visiting with parents, relatives, and guardians in my new office that I first became aware of the great effort that had gone into enabling these Hispanic youths to benefit from the relative peace and opportunity of life in the United States. The parents and guardians talked not only of the severe hardships inherent in escaping the economic scarcity and political terror that characterized their situation in Central America, but also of the ongoing hardships in the new land, where they had entered the lowest levels of the occupational structure. They spoke little or no English, and many of them were doomed to remain in marginal legal positions so long as they lacked the required documentation for residency.

The Tensions of Teaching

In the course of my research in the schools, I worked productively with seven teachers. When one of them, Mr. Bozza, heard that an anthropologist was doing research on the lives of new immigrants from Central America, he approached me and made it clear that he had a lot of ideas on the subject and was anxious to talk to me about them. We went on to spend hours discussing his profession, the school, the immigrant kids, and their future. It was easy to work harmoniously with the teachers, but for the most part the relationships were impersonal. Nevertheless, when I began spending less time in their classrooms, they acknowledged that they missed my presence.

For some of the teachers, who were psychologically detached from their work, teaching was essentially a "nine-to-five" enterprise. And there were some teachers with whom I became acquainted who seemed somewhat resentful. Ms. Garcia, herself a Hispanic, told me that her primary job was to "housebreak the little immigrants who come down from the Central American mountains." Still others expressed fear and helplessness. They often seemed in a hurry to leave the school. Most teachers complained that they were underpaid, overworked, and lacked status. Many seemed defensive about their profession: they felt too much was expected of them. They could not be held responsible for all the evils of the inner city, one informant said. Some felt specifically that the press and the local government blamed them for many inner-city problems. They told of countless sad encounters with administrators and students. Indeed, the teacher who was a dedicated professional seemed to be a rare species. As my work progressed and I became more intimate with the schools and their teachers, I realized that the impressions I gained from repeated observations of individual teachers were applicable on a general level to both schools.

There was evidence, too, of the social ills that plague our society in general. One morning, as I drew close to an aide to ask a question, I noticed that his breath reeked of alcohol. A student later told me too that one of the hall guards was regularly "high" on marijuana. Another immigrant student reported that the realization that illicit drugs were so much a part of school life diminished her view of education. It was evident that many Central American students were disturbed by the many outside pressures intruding on their learning environment.

Overall, the teachers suffered from a sense of helplessness. Work in the inner-city high school was too stressful, they said; they were suffering from "burnout." Gang violence and lack of respect were primary concerns. All the teachers, at one time or another, reported being physically overworked. One teacher looked overwhelmed with classes of as many as 37 students. She had been trained to teach classes of up to 20 or 25 students. Her aide, absent most of the semester, was suing the school district over a disability she had incurred on the job. The school district had decided that there would be no replacement until the case was settled in court. In the meantime, classes had to go on with or without an aide.

Among these seven teachers whom I came to know, only two seemed genuinely concerned about the well-being of their students and would intervene, for example, on behalf of students whom the counseling office had enrolled in low-level classes that they had already taken in their country of origin. Mr. Bozza earned the strong dislike of Joaquin's bilingual counselor for regularly speaking on behalf of students and involving himself in their personal lives. When he heard that Ernesto had been sleeping in a car because he had no place to live, Mr. Bozza took him into his own home while the youth looked for a more permanent residence. It was Mr. Bozza too who pushed Ernesto to apply to the university and helped him through the unfamiliar process until Ernesto was finally accepted. In short, he cared.

This is not to imply that most of the other teachers were hostile to their students. In fact, most of them indicated that they enjoyed the immigrant students, whose conduct was far superior to that of their American-born students. Two teachers noted that they would never go back to the regular classrooms—that is, non-bilingual/non-ESL—at an inner-city school, where they would have to face mostly American-born minority students who were unruly. Two ESL teachers noted also that it was a joy to see how motivated the immigrant students were to learn English. One said, "I don't have to fight them every step of the way," referring to her prior experiences in teaching English to American students.

Mr. Ramos, another ESL teacher, repeated that he "loved" teaching the immigrant youths. He had taught for four years in a school with a large Black and Chicano population, and the differences were "unbelievable." I asked him to explain. "Well," he said, "it has to do with attitudes. . . . The Chicano kids are so *macho* they just can't sit in the classroom for 50 minutes. It's not macho. If you are a macho, you are out with the guys." It was a pleasant surprise to find out that recent immigrants were eager to learn, particularly the English language.

The teachers routinely reported lacking even the most basic teaching materials. Mr. Bozza noted with some anger that he had to teach algebra with books that were totally out-of-date, as far as he was concerned. Yet ironically, the fact that U.S. schools loaned books at all—however "out-of-date"—was pointed out more than once by the immigrant students, parents, and guardians as evidence of the greater opportunities available in this country. In Central America, some said, they had to buy the books, which they could not afford to do.

The Burden to Achieve

As the research progressed, I was increasingly impressed by the fact that so many of the new arrivals remained in school at all. The schools provided a learning environment that was far from ideal. Some of the teachers were outright incompetent, or "not fully there." The pressures on the immigrants to work were great. Yet, they remained in school and some succeeded. Five went on to enroll in college.

Other Central American students, particularly the younger ones, seemed to succumb to the effects of the legacy of terror in Central America, bad and overcrowded schools, the need to work, poor living conditions, lack of proper parental/community supervision, or peer-group pressures. We shall return to these issues later. Some students reported an overwhelming sense of boredom brought on by pointless, repetitive tasks in the classroom. During the two weeks just prior to the Christmas break, an ESL teacher spent her entire school day singing Christmas songs to the students in English. The new immigrants could not understand the point. They sat as if stupefied, hour after hour, as the teacher sang the same songs over and over again. It was as if she had run out of topics to teach. She seemed anxious for a vacation and rationalized her activities by saying that the immigrants "must learn American folklore."

Some younger immigrant students cut classes and began to lose interest in school. Others just dropped out of school to devote themselves fully to work, to earn money to help their relatives, particularly those left behind in Central America.

The students themselves, particularly the older ones, remained keenly aware of the hardships their parents had endured. Some informants could not help feeling that these sacrifices had been made so that they could get ahead in a more affluent society. These feelings put definite psychological burdens to achieve on the youngsters. The parents and other relatives wanted the students to stay and do well in school. They said the youngsters now had a chance they never had: to study and become somebody. In my conversations with parents it became evident that they gained a vicarious sense of accomplishment through the efforts of their children. Their most cherished wish was that the children would enter college and become *universitarios*. The statement *Nosotros queremos que nuestro hijo llegue a ser alguien* ("We want our son to become somebody") was often repeated to me throughout my work. Vlach found a similar pattern of "goals of future achievement," particularly through the children, in her study of recent immigrant families from Guatemala (1984: 232).

After six months in the two schools, I had amassed a great deal of data from patterns of interethnic communication and miscommunication in the classrooms, inappropriate classroom assignments and student initiatives to circumvent them, parental reflections on why they had decided to leave their country, and how the students viewed their current lives and future in the United States.

Sensitized by the suggestions of the ethnographic recording, I began systematically to interview students on a standard set of issues, ranging from length of stay in the United States to more hypothetical questions aimed at eliciting "free associations" such as, "Suppose a cousin of yours comes here from Central America and asks you to tell him/her how life is in this country, what would you tell him/her?" In the course of the next few months, I talked with students in the morning and worked with parents in the afternoon. Most students took part eagerly in the interviews. They wanted to talk, to be heard.

Research Methods

In the two schools there were approximately 600 Central American youths who had entered the United States within the five years prior to the research.* Of these, I consciously eliminated from consideration those whose family background was more upper-status, that is, upper-level professional and business, which accounted for approximately 40 youths, mostly Nicaraguans. I reached my projected quota of collecting from the Central American population 50 full cases involving both the youngsters and their families. In addition, I maintained contact with many of the remaining youngsters and their parents through my work as community liaison.

I made the selections as nearly as possible in the proportion that each of the three Central American countries was represented in the schools. Thirty-three of my informants were from El Salvador (ES), nine from Guatemala (G), and eight from Nicaragua (N). For reasons any anthropologist who has done research among Latin Americans would understand, I had greater access to the young men than to the young women: in my sample there were thirty males (M) and twenty females (F), all in the 14–19 age group. Clearly, this was not a statistically random sample. Rather, as is true in most anthropological work, the collecting of data was influenced by the availability and willingness of those contacted. Two or three of the immigrants refused to be interviewed, and there were seven who specifically asked to be interviewed. The work as parent/community liaison put me

---

* I have not considered the experiences of other Spanish-speaking immigrant students from Central America who had been in the United States for more than five years.

in daily contact with parents, relatives, and friends as well with a number of organizations providing services to the community.

Ernesto* left his native Usulután in El Salvador one morning in early 1981. He was just 15 years old when he embarked, alone, upon the long and dangerous journey north. He had concluded that there was no future for him in his own land. Increasing political violence and economic scarcity made his country, in his words, "a place where it is a sin to be young." There was simply no immunity from the escalating crossfire. His father, mother, and younger brother José stayed behind in El Salvador.

After establishing himself in the United States, Ernesto remained constantly concerned about his family's fate. He told me that his brother José would be considered a valuable asset to either side of the Salvadorean conflict: "He is young and one of the best students in school." Ernesto's project now was to bring José to the safety of the United States, and eventually his parents would follow too.

During his last year in high school in the United States, Ernesto worked full-time, well into the night, in a restaurant and went to school during the day. Every month, part of his salary went home to his parents, "to help them survive there," he said. How much he sent them depended on how much he made, his own current needs, and his saving plans. Upon graduating from high school, Ernesto was accepted into one of the great West Coast universities. When autumn came, he could not enroll because he lacked the cash to supplement a scholarship stipend he had won. He felt disappointed but not defeated. He continued to work at the restaurant and began to explore other sources of aid. By winter he had saved enough to be able to begin classes at the university. The day he learned that he could finally begin, Ernesto told me, "Now I will *really* be able to help my family."

Angel left San Salvador in 1981. Also 15 years old, he came to the United States with his mother, Rafaela, and an older sister, Ana. Rafaela had decided to join her sister, who had been living in the United States for more than a decade. In El Salvador, she had feared that her Angel would eventually become a target of the aggressive recruiting campaigns of either the military or the guerrillas. Had they stayed, she said, her children's future

---

* All names have been changed to protect the privacy of my informants.

would probably be a repetition of her own life of hard work, limited opportunity, and no education. Four years later, when I came into contact with this family, Rafaela was cleaning houses and Ana was working in a restaurant. They did not want Angel to work; he had to dedicate himself fully to study. Upon successfully completing high school, Angel was accepted into a West Coast university. Rafaela glowed with pride. "He'll be the first *universitario* in the family," she said with joy. Rafaela herself had been forced to interrupt her studies while still in elementary school in El Salvador. Her hands were needed for work.

Amadeo left Managua, Nicaragua, in 1983, escaping the military draft when he was 17 years old. His parents and older sister had to stay behind: the family could afford to send only one of the two youngsters out of Nicaragua, and Amadeo was chosen. Young men, he said, as if apologizing, are more likely "to be taken away by the army." When I met Amadeo, he was living in the United States with a maternal uncle, the uncle's wife, and their three children. Amadeo went to school during the day and worked with his uncle in a warehouse well into the night. Throughout 1984, he remained concerned about the situation in his native Nicaragua. His sister, who still lived there with his parents, could not find the funds needed to study at the local university. Amadeo was seeking ways to earn sufficient money to bring her to the United States. "Here she would become an architect," he said once.

José, Estela, and Pedro had stayed in their native Guatemala with their maternal grandmother after their mother had departed alone on the uncertain journey to the United States. She was escaping economic misery and a drunken, abusive husband. Some years later, when she felt sufficiently secure, she sent for her children to join her. When I first met them, she worked as a maid, six days a week. Upon their arrival, she immediately enrolled the children in school. She wanted them to get an education and one day "be somebody," as she put it. All three children made the school's honor roll during their first semester.

From prior research on the school functioning of Hispanic Americans (Suarez-Orozco 1986; 1987*a*; 1987*c*), I had become especially interested in the relative adaptation of given ethnic groups to American schooling. I had identified five areas that seemed to warrant closer study: (1) the influence of language and cultural differences on school performance; (2) the influence of parents and teachers on school performance; versus (3) the influence of peer reference groups on behavior, in and out of school, and how it affected school performance; (4) the relative presence or absence of internalized patterns of achievement motivation; and (5) the influence on school performance of specific shared perceptions of the occupational opportunity structure.

Not all of these issues have received equal attention. My focus was particularly the classroom and family atmospheres, the internalized concerns of students that seemed most salient in this particular sample, and their emerging perceptions of opportunity in the new society. In future work, I hope to use this study to enable me to make comparisons to other groups. Information concerning school functioning came from direct observation in the school settings, from formal interviews on specific topics, and by indirectly eliciting data on attitudes and interpersonal and family concerns through the Thematic Apperception Test (TAT). I also conducted a number of special interviews with key informants who were teachers and staff in the schools, as well as with active members of community organizations working with Central American immigrants. I also had access to the students' school records through my work as a school employee.

The Thematic Apperception Test proved to be extremely valuable in revealing attitudes about topics that would have been inappropriate to approach directly. For example, the stories elicited by the tests reflected a continuing underlying concern both with the violence and terror experienced in Central America and with a sense of self-sacrifice and obligation that bonded family members together. I collected over 400 TAT stories from my informants, not as a tool for individual psycho-diagnosis, but rather as a medium enabling me to elicit certain normative interpersonal concerns. In the chapters that follow, I use the results of these tests and interviews to analyze the factors that contributed to the adaptation of the Central American immigrant youths.

Hispanics in the United States

THE FEDERAL CENSUS for 1987 reported about 18.8 million persons of "Spanish origin" residing in the United States. According to census analyses, Hispanics are the nation's second-largest minority group, making up 7.9 percent of the total population.* With a fertility rate 60 percent higher than the non-Hispanic average and continuing emigration from Mexico and Central and South America, they are also the fastest-growing minority group in the United States. From 1950 to 1980 the number of Hispanics in the United States grew by about 250 percent, compared with growth of less than 50 percent for the total population. Hispanic immigration also has been on the rise since the 1950's: 956,000 Hispanics, 1950–59; 1.3 million, 1960–69; 1.4 million, 1970–79 (Davis et al. 1983: 20). These figures fail to include the millions of Hispanics who have crossed the southern border without legal documentation.†

Hispanics of Mexican descent, or Mexican Americans, continue to be the largest subgroup, numbering 11.8 million (63 percent of all Hispanics). In addition, in 1987 there were 2.3 million mainland Puerto Ricans (12.5 percent); 1 million Cuban Americans (5.5 percent), and 3.7 million "other Hispanics" (19 percent), which include Hispanics of Central and South American origin. Although Hispanic Americans reside in every state of the Union, more than two-thirds of them live in four states: California (about 4.5 million), Texas (about 3 million), New York (about

---

* Blacks were the largest minority group, at 11.7 percent of the total U.S. population in 1980.

† For a consideration of the various estimates of how many illegal aliens there are in the United States, see Cross and Sandos 1981: 150–54; Davis et al. 1983: 27; Lewis 1980: 31–40; Lancaster and Scheuren 1977; see also Portes 1978.

2 million), and Florida (about 1 million). Contrary to common belief, Hispanic Americans today generally do not live in rural areas. In fact, 88 percent of all Hispanics live in metropolitan areas, compared with about 75 percent of the total American population (Davis et al. 1983: 13).

Hispanic Americans are younger than the U.S. population as a whole. In 1980, for example, their median age was 22.1 years, compared to 30.1 years for the total U.S. population, and 32 percent of all Hispanics were under 15 years of age (HPDP 1984: 2.29).* Demographers associate these figures with a relatively high fertility ratio among Hispanics of 2.5 children per woman, as opposed to the 1.8 children per woman in the U.S. population as a whole. Also, more than one-third of all Hispanic immigrants entering the United States in the 1970's were in the 20–34 age bracket, "the prime childbearing ages" (Davis et al. 1983: 10).

Hispanics tend to be poorer than the majority of the population. Their median family income in 1979 was $14,711, as against $20,840 for Whites. On the basis of census figures, it is estimated that 24.7 percent of Hispanics in the United States live below the poverty level. They fared better than blacks, 30.2 percent of whom live below the poverty level. The income level of Hispanics in the 1980's census was about 70 percent of that for the U.S. population as a whole. In fact, over the past three decades a 30 percent difference in income levels has persisted between Hispanics and the population at large (HPDP 1984: 2.15, 24).

The jobless rate among Hispanics is "typically 40 to 50 percent higher than the overall unemployment rate." In 1982, about 15.2 percent of Hispanic workers remained out of work. Hispanics tend to be concentrated in lower-paid and lesser-skilled occupations. For example, more than 75 percent of the employed women of Mexican American, Puerto Rican American, and Cuban American descent were employed in three of the lowest-paid categories: as clerical workers, machine operators, and service workers (Davis et al. 1983: 35). This figure obtained likewise for my informants from Central America. Nationwide figures show Hispanics to be overrepresented in blue-collar occupations, with a 45.4 percent presence, compared with 31.9 per-

---

* For a general profile of the age and sex composition of Hispanic Americans, see Davis et al. 1983: 9–13.

cent of the total population. Conversely, only 34.5 percent of the Hispanics are white-collar workers, compared with 51.9 percent of the total U.S. population (HPDP 1984: 2.26).

Some Comparative Considerations of Hispanic American Subgroups

Although it is useful to employ the term "Hispanic," one should not thereby minimize the differences separating the various subgroups who remain distinct populations, both historically and demographically. Mexican Americans, the largest and fastest-growing Hispanic subgroup, are themselves heterogeneous. Historically they include not only those who lived in the Western territories before the coming of the Anglo-Europeans but also the recent immigrants, whose number has been on the rise since the 1950's. In 1951–60, 299,811 Mexican immigrants entered the United States with full documentation; in 1961–70 453,937; and in 1971–80, 640,294 (see *Statistical Yearbook of the Immigration and Naturalization Service* 1984).* They trace their descent variously, from Spanish and Mestizo to a number of native Indian origins. About 41.6 percent of all Mexican Americans (3.6 million) reside in California, and more than 31.5 percent of them (about 2.7 million) reside in Texas. Their median age is 21.4 years, as opposed to 30.1 years for the total U.S. population. Continuing immigration from Mexico and relatively high fertility rates assure that the Mexican American population will continue to grow fast (HPDP 1984: 2.29, 36).

In 1979 the median family income for Mexican Americans was $15,200, considerably less than for the entire U.S. population. According to 1980 U.S. census figures, only 31.2 percent of the Mexican Americans occupied white-collar positions, compared with 51.9 percent of the total U.S. population.

In numbers, Cuban Americans are the smallest of the Hispanic subgroups. Most are relatively recent arrivals in the United States, the majority having come in the last 20 years. In the 1950's, 78,948 Cubans entered the United States as immigrants.

---

* Some key studies of Mexican immigration to the United States are Portes and Bach 1985; Cornelius 1982, 1981, 1978; Cross and Sandos 1981; Tylor 1976; Gamio 1971; Samora 1971.

In the 1960's, following the defeat (in late 1958) of Fulgencio Batista and Fidel Castro's ascent to power, 208,536 Cubans entered the United States. And in 1971–80, some 264,863 Cubans came to the United States. The most recent arrivals are the so-called Marielitos, some 120,000 in number, who entered the United States in the 1980's. About 85 percent of the Cuban American population resides in Florida. They have a median age of 33.5 years, with relatively few births (Portes and Bach 1985: 72–110). Cuban Americans are the most affluent Hispanics, with a median family income of $17,500 in 1979 and, for "a relatively high" 29.8 percent of families an annual income of $25,000 or more. They are more concentrated in white-collar occupations (41.7 percent) and have the lowest unemployment rate of the Hispanic subgroups. "In summary, Cuban Americans are the oldest, highest-earning, most geographically concentrated, and most white-collar-employed of the major Hispanic population groups" (HPDP 1984: 2.44).

Puerto Ricans living on the mainland of the United States have the youngest median age, the most city dwellers, and the poorest economic circumstances of any Hispanic group. According to 1980 census figures, their median age was 20.7 years, and their median family income (according to 1979 figures) a low $9,900 per year. They suffer the highest unemployment rate of the subgroups (see Davis et al. 1983: 35), with employment concentrated in low-income service and blue-collar occupations.

"Other Spanish/Hispanic" appeared as a category in the 1980 U.S. census. According to the Hispanic Policy Development Project, this rubric includes Latin American immigrants, a refugee professional class, Central American economic refugees, part Hispanics (the children of a marriage between a Hispanic and a non-Hispanic), "mixed Hispanics" (the children of a marriage between members of different Hispanic subgroups), and Hispanos in the Southwest, who have lived in the United States since the last century (HPDP 1984: 2.48). This statistical grouping is hopelessly heterogeneous, including as it does U.S.-born Hispanics and a variety of recent arrivals from Central and South America. Taken together, the "other Hispanics" are a young population with a median age of 23.3 years and an annual median family income for 1979 of $15,500. This group is apt to be employed in white-collar jobs (43.6 percent). Of the "other Hispanics," 38.0 percent worked in blue-collar jobs, 16.6 percent in service jobs, and 1.7 percent in farm jobs. More than 3 million Hispanics do not use the Spanish language at home (Davis et al. 1983: 4). They are, however, unified in the dominant culture by an Anglo-American attitude of denigration with respect to all inhabitants of lands "South of the Border." Immigrant Hispanics share with all immigrants the dream of a better future despite a special history of subordination vis-à-vis an expanding Anglo-Saxon world. For the Mexican Americans and the Puerto Ricans in particular that experience has tended to create specific issues of identity not shared by the new arrivals.

In any consideration of educational functioning in American schools, one must keep in mind the various historical, structural, and situational factors that apply to both Hispanic and non-Hispanic populations, immigrant and nonimmigrant populations, and White and non-White populations. Teachers and other students tend to lump children of various groups into American folk categories by language and cultural background, physical characteristics, and social class. The effects of all these variables, which are operative in the American classroom, must be kept in mind. In addition, we must examine issues of self and social identity that determine responses to external attitudes. The complex interactions of external attitudes with internal features of psychocultural identities all help to explain why some Hispanics give up on school while others remain and succeed, often seemingly against all odds.

Research on the Educational Functioning of Hispanic Americans

The functioning of Hispanics within U.S. schools has garnered increasing attention in the last two decades.* There is strong evidence that Hispanics as a group lag far behind the majority population in any array of standard educational measurements. In a major statistical document entitled *The Condition of Education for Hispanic Americans* (1980), George H. Brown and his co-authors

---

* For recent overviews, see Suarez-Orozco 1987a, c, 1986; Walker 1987; Lefkowitz 1985; HPDP 1984: vol. 1; Brown et al. 1980; Fernandez and Marenco 1980; Carter and Segura 1979; Benitez and Villareal 1979.

describe the major quantitative aspects of schooling for Hispanics. On the question of school enrollment patterns, they report that "considering the relative youth of the Hispanic population, school enrollment data point to three disturbing trends in the education of Hispanics: Hispanic children enroll in schools at rates lower than those for non-Hispanic students, they fall behind their classmates in progressing through school, and their attrition rates are higher than those of non-Hispanic students." The authors report that these trends begin early and that the gap between the Hispanic students and their White counterparts tends to increase with age. For example, school enrollment data show that only 56.7 percent of Hispanics aged three to six are enrolled in school, compared with 64.6 percent of White children in the same age category (Brown et al. 1980: 4, 20). For the 18–24 age range, the gap increases, with 28.5 percent of all Whites enrolled in school, compared with 20.1 percent of Hispanics.

Hispanics in the 14–19 group were twice as likely as Whites not to have completed high school. Those who did remain in school were older and less likely than their White classmates to enroll in college preparatory programs. Although Hispanic and White seniors demonstrated similar homework habits, Hispanics received lower grades than their White counterparts. Hispanic high school seniors participated less than their White counterparts in an array of extracurricular activities (Brown et al. 1980: 65, 67, 69, 77). The White/Hispanic difference appears enormous when we consider that almost 25 percent of the Mexican American population, compared to less than 4 percent of the non-Hispanic, has less than five years of schooling. This Mexican American percentage is much higher than that of any other Hispanic subgroups (Brown et al. 1980: 20; see also Maestas 1981; Knowlton 1979)—further evidence that there are important differences among the various Hispanic subgroups.

Socioeconomic status (SES), although an important factor in educational achievement, does not seem to explain the White/Hispanic gap in educational performance. Brown and his colleagues note that at "all income levels Hispanic students were more likely than Whites to fall behind in school." Although middle-class Hispanics tend to do better in school than lower-class Hispanics, they tend to perform below their middle-class

White counterparts. The same is true when the educational attainment of parents is taken into consideration: "Hispanics fell behind [in school] more than Whites regardless of the educational attainment of their parents" (Brown et al. 1980: 91, 93), which seems to suggest that SES and parental educational attainment cannot by themselves explain the White/Hispanic gap in educational performance. That gap spills across class and SES barriers.

A more recent document by the Hispanic Policy Development Project, entitled *"Make Something Happen": Hispanics and Urban School Reform* (1984), essentially corroborates these findings. "The fundamental finding of the National Commission on Secondary Education for Hispanics is that a shocking proportion of this generation of Hispanics is being wasted." The commission concluded that although the majority of Hispanics enter high school with educational and career aspirations as high as those of the majority population, and although Hispanic parents are "deeply concerned about schooling," Hispanic students continue to fail in school at alarming rates. Furthermore, 40 percent of Hispanic students leave school before the tenth grade. Nationwide, at least 45 percent of the Mexican American and Puerto Rican students who do enter high school never graduate, compared to only 17 percent of White youths. In the New York metropolitan area as many as 80 percent of Hispanic students drop out of school. Over two-thirds of all Hispanics are enrolled in schools with student bodies that are more than 50 percent minority. Hispanics usually attend schools that are "overcrowded, or are poorly equipped, or have lower per-pupil budgets than other schools in adjacent areas" (HPDP 1984: 1.1, 9, 10, 23). Both Joaquin and Jefferson High fit this description well.

The HPDP report also notes that in 1980 not only were Hispanic male students more likely than White or Black students to work full-time, but they also averaged more hours of work per week while enrolled in school. These students reported to HPDP that the need to work "in order to contribute to the support of their families" was related to their school problems, as was indeed the case among my informants (HPDP 1984: 1.23).

Those Hispanics who remained in school tended to enroll in a less academic, more vocational program of study. Hispanic achievement scores in standard tests have generally been below the national average. For example, the nationwide scores for 9-, 13-, and 17-year-old Hispanic students in science, mathematics, reading, social studies, and career and occupational development were significantly below the national average (at the 0.05 level), and even lower than the average for White students (Brown et al. 1980: 97). In 1982, only 43 percent of those Hispanics who graduated from high school went on to enroll in college, a figure three percentage points below the 1972 figure. Once in college, Hispanics lagged behind Whites in a variety of measurements. Of every 100 Hispanics who entered college in 1972, for example, only 13 had completed their baccalaureates by 1976 (HPDP 1984: 1.24). Throughout the 1970's the gap between Hispanic and White school noncompletion rates remained relatively stable, with Hispanics failing to complete high school about twice as often as Whites.

Upon close scrutiny we find among the Hispanic American subgroups certain heuristically important differences in educational functioning. Research on this phenomenon, which appears to be related to the nature of Hispanic heterogeneity, has been scanty because of the limited amount of data on school differences among Hispanic subgroups; more research on this topic is needed.

The record to date suggests that mainland Puerto Ricans and Mexican Americans tend to lag behind Cuban Americans and the "other Hispanics." According to some measurements, these differences are marked. For example, HPDP reports that whereas 21.15 percent of the Mexican American sophomores dropped out of school in the year 1982, only 11.4 percent of the "other Hispanic" students dropped out that same year (HPDP 1984: 2.57). For the U.S. sophomore population as a whole the dropout figure was 13.7 percent, or 2.3 percentage points *above* the "other Hispanic" figure. That is, sophomore Hispanics of Central and South American origin dropped out of school at a rate lower than the average for the total U.S. population. Davis and his co-authors similarly conclude that Cuban Americans and the more recent immigrants from Central and South America tend to be better educated than Mexican Americans and mainland Puerto Ricans. Likewise, Brown and his associates report that "Puerto

Rican and Mexican Americans had much higher noncompletion rates [in high school] than the other Hispanic subgroup." Their data show that whereas over 30 percent of the mainland Puerto Rican high-school students did not complete school, fewer than 15 percent of the Cubans and "other Hispanic" did not complete high school (Davis et al. 1983: 29; Brown et al. 1980: 101).

These data seem to support the contentions of John Ogbu and his associates that, on the whole, "immigrant minorities" such as the Chinese, Japanese, Punjabi Sikhs, and South and Central Americans tend to do better in school in the United States than do "castelike" minorities such as the American Indians, Black Americans, mainland Puerto Ricans, and Mexican Americans (see Ogbu 1983, 1984, 1985; Ogbu and Matute-Bianchi 1986; Gibson 1983, 1987, in press).

Before defining these terms (castelike, immigrant) more precisely, I should mention that there are a number of theoretically important reasons why the recent immigrants from Central America under consideration here may not fully reflect the immigrant paradigm described by Ogbu and his associates, owing to questions about the legal status of large numbers of recent arrivals and to other variables that I will discuss later.

Minority Status and School Functioning

The research presented here was conceived in reference to what I see as two essentially complementary approaches to the study of minority status and educational functioning in complex societies. They are George De Vos's model of minority status and psychosocial adaptation and John Ogbu's cultural-ecological approach to the problem of minority status and education in plural societies. Yet other models have been put forth by anthropologists, sociologists, psychologists, educators, and others to explain why Hispanics, particularly Mexican Americans and Puerto Rican Americans, continue to fail in U.S. schools at such alarmingly high rates. Four major explanatory traditions can be identified in the scholarly literature: (1) biological determinism; (2) cultural deprivation; (3) the emphasis on "discontinuity" between the minority Hispanic and the majority culture; and (4) a psychosocial approach.

Biological Determinism

Although still alive in various forms in the work of Jensen (1969) Eysenck (1971), and others, the biological tradition today seems to carry little weight in the debate over the problematic school performance of certain minority groups.* The biological tradition is historically the oldest of the explanatory models under consideration and, upon close scrutiny, probably the least illuminating on the nature of the problem. Since major books, articles, and symposia have been devoted to the complex question of intelligence, inheritance, and group achievement, I attempt to explore only certain findings relevant to the poor performance of Hispanics in U.S. schools. The biological tradition assumes that intelligence, however defined, is largely inherited and varies from group to group.† Furthermore, biological intelligence can be measured by IQ tests, whose scores can predict future academic achievement.

Hispanic children in the United States, mostly Mexican and Mexican American, have been tested from the beginning of the century and found wanting. A number of the early comparative studies among Mexican, Mexican American, and Puerto Rican children argued that shared and inherited racial characteristics accounted for the low scores.‡ The assumptions behind these biological arguments, however, are seriously flawed. The construction of hierarchical groups by measurement of their "increasing complexity" was the natural outgrowth of nineteenth-century evolutionary theories. Early theorists such as Lewis H. Morgan suggested that differences among peoples could be ordered in an evolutionary sequence of development from "savagery" and "barbarism" to "civilization." Civilization was the aim of history. According to this model, human history unfolded by some obscure design, moving all peoples, albeit at different rates, toward a state of civilization. In retrospect, the

---

* For reviews of this tradition, see Trueba 1987; Gould 1981; Carter and Segura 1979; Montagu 1975; and Ogbu 1974.

† According to Jensen (1969), as much as 80 percent of intelligence is inherited.

‡ For discussion (both pro and con) of this issue, see Urrabazo 1985; Gould 1981; Ogbu 1978: 218–19; Montagu 1975: 1–18; Jensen 1969; Garth and Johnson 1934; Garretson 1928.

naïveté of these models seems striking. The yardstick used to measure increasing complexity put a premium on traits that the European model-makers themselves possessed and valued. The emphasis given to cities (civilization), or to writing, or to technological complexity predictably placed European elites at the apex of most such scales. Commonly, the British, German, and French elites were on top, leaving the peoples of tribal Africa, Native America, and Australia at the lowest level (savagery), with European peasants, Mediterraneans, and Near and Far Easterns somewhere in between (barbarians) (see Lowie 1937: 54–67). These arbitrary and scientifically untenable models were also invoked in debates on innate differences in intellectual capacities among human groups.

How "others," usually Africans, Native Americans, and non-Whites, were determined to be intellectually inferior to the White European makes a sad, if at times absurd, chapter in the history of science.* It is impossible to review here the various faces of anthropometric contributions to the hierarchical classification of man according to alleged shared, fixed, and inherited traits. Suffice it to note that craniometry and IQ testing, whatever their other merits, were often used to cloak bigotry and prejudice with the mantle of science. More specifically, the results of such intelligence testing were cited to explain high failure and retardation rates among Mexican American students.

To date, no one really knows what intelligence is. And although we can refer to certain problem-solving capacities, it belittles human complexity to suggest that diversities in human talent can be reduced to the monolithic process of inheritance. The test researchers themselves are quick to point out that the word *intelligence*, as defined by them, is an operational concept, nothing more than "that which an IQ test measures." Of more immediate concern here is the use of such tests in cross-cultural research, particularly among ethnic minorities such as Hispanic Americans. The fact remains that both Blacks and Hispanics have regularly scored below Whites in IQ tests. Whatever the explanation for these differences, there is currently little recourse to biology for enlightenment.

Ogbu has pointed to some specific shortcomings of intelli-

---

* For a dynamic history of the "mismeasure of man," see Gould 1981.

gence testing when it is used cross-culturally or among ethnic minorities. He notes that an IQ test rests on the assumption that it taps mental abilities that are "more or less" universally found in all human populations, with some variations according to genetic endowment. Even if we assume that these units (cognitive abilities or potentials) have a more or less universal distribution, the ethnographic record has made clear that different cultural and ecological settings encourage the development of very different cognitive skills and abilities. Furthermore, as Ogbu has noted, "The ability theory of cognition makes no allowance for the fact that IQ tests may evoke in subjects from different cultural backgrounds cognitive skills and strategies different from those intended by the testers" (Ogbu 1978: 30; Berry and Dasen 1974; De Vos and Hippler 1969). People of varying cultural backgrounds may have more developed skills and abilities not deemed worthy of measurement by the testers, or they may undervalue the abilities and skills deemed worthy of measurement by the testers, or they may respond to the test in a manner incompatible with the intentions of the tester.

In summary, the poor school performance of Hispanic Americans was first framed in the context of testing instruments devised to measure allegedly innate and shared cognitive abilities and skills. Questionable results were in turn invoked to give the impression that Hispanic children did poorly in schools because they were innately less intelligent than children belonging to the majority culture. The assessment by Carter and Segura is well stated: "Lower innate intelligence is no longer ascribed to Mexican American children. Although IQ scores may be low, most school people explain this phenomenon in terms of environment, the inadequacy of available psychometric instruments, or both" (Carter and Segura 1979: 96; see also Urrabazo 1985: 15–19; Ogbu 1978: 54–65).

Cultural Deprivation

Arguments based on the influence of cultural background on classroom performance often emphasize distinct yet related themes. During the 1960's the contention flourished that certain cultural backgrounds were inferior because they failed to inculcate in children the basic tools required for successful school functioning. In brief, a number of scholars have argued that among certain minorities such as Blacks and Hispanics, the cultural tradition itself is responsible for high rates of school failure. Bloom, Davis, and Hess write that the root of the problem can "be traced to . . . experiences in the home which do not transmit the cultural patterns necessary for the types of learning characteristic of the schools and the larger society" (1965: 4). Throughout these narratives there is an implicit notion that certain minorities fail to foster "normal" development. Ogbu has noted, for example, that "according to the cultural deprivation theory, children are culturally deprived when they come from home and neighborhood environments that do not provide them with adequately organized stimulation for normal development" (Ogbu 1978: 44). In the literature on Hispanic Americans, devoted chiefly to mainland Puerto Ricans and Mexican Americans, cultural deprivation emerged as a popular explanation for poor school performance. Heller, for example, wrote, "The kind of socialization Mexican American children receive at home is not conducive to the development of capacities needed for advancement in a dynamic industrialized society. This type of upbringing creates stumbling blocks to future advancement by stressing values that hinder mobility—family ties, honor, masculinity, and living in the present—and by neglecting the values that are conducive to it, achievement, independence, and deferred gratification" (Heller 1966: 34–35). This model would suggest that the Mexican American family hinders school achievement by creating asphyxiating "ties" that retard independence and thus achievement.

According to the cultural deprivation tradition, poor socialization techniques are evident in the fact that Hispanic children are less stimulated linguistically than White children. For example, Killian argues that Hispanic American kindergarten and first-graders are "deficient on the input side of communicative skills, especially in understanding sentences and pictures" (1971: 42). Others have noted that culturally deprived children fail in school because they lack "an educational tradition" in the home and have few books, as well as being subject to "poor health, improper diet, frequent moving, and noisy TV-ridden homes" (Riessman 1962: 4). The blame must be placed somewhere. The cultural deprivation model served as the theoretical framework for the so-called war on poverty programs. Given that minority children entered school somewhat handicapped by their cultural background, the argument continued, a fundamental role of the school should be to correct or repair the cultural damage with such compensatory and/or remedial programs as flourished in the 1960's.

There are a number of serious weaknesses in this explanatory tradition. First, a somewhat arbitrary list of traits hardly constitutes a culture in the anthropological sense of the term. Culture is no more a sum of traits than personality is a sum of instincts or drives.* Second, as Trueba (1987) and others have pointed out, the cultural deprivation "rationale coheres beautifully to the American brand of ethnocentrism: Minority problems are caused by *their* peculiar form of culture" (Carter and Segura 1979: 77; their emphasis). Third, there is a serious fallacy in this tradition. Although its point of departure is minority non-learning in school, the model does not explain why minority children learn their own culture and language so successfully that it interferes with learning in the classroom (see Ogbu 1978: 46; Gottfried 1973: 275). A major weakness of this model is that it seems to utilize certain White, middle-class traits as the yardstick for "normalcy," branding as pathological any ethnic departures from this preconceived, arbitrary standard.†

Cultural Conflicts and Discontinuities in Communication

Increasing disenchantment with some aspects of the cultural deprivation model and praxis led scholars to examine more carefully the nature of the conflicts that may be preventing large numbers of students from successfully achieving in school. We shall examine two distinct approaches to the causes of the problem: a "culture conflict" tradition that permeated the scholarly literature throughout the 1970's, and a more recent approach, which emphasizes certain "discontinuities" between the minority student and the school (majority) environment. The latter approach commonly examines how cognitive, linguistic, and dis-

---

* For a discussion of the concept of culture utilized in contemporary social science, see Geertz 1973: 3–30.

† For overviews of this model, see Ogbu 1978: 44–46; Carter and Segura 1979: 75–78.

course strategies vary across ethnic groups, often leading to culturally based misunderstandings and minority nonlearning in schools.

The conflict approach argues that certain misunderstandings emerge in the process of ethnic interaction and lead directly to interethnic conflict and nonlearning on the part of minority students. In this case, as opposed to the cultural deprivation explanation, conflicts are based on the Anglo-Saxon teachers' ignorance and intolerance of ethnic linguistic and cognitive styles, values, worldview, and so forth. The problem according to this tradition is with the teachers, who, in the final analysis, are unable to understand ethnically distinct students. For example, the Hispanic cultural syndrome *machismo* has been singled out as a cause of conflict in the classroom, particularly for Mexican American adolescent males. As Johnson notes, *macho* behavior, particularly manliness and self-reliance, may create conflicts as teachers try to discipline adolescent boys in the classroom (1970: 71). A failure to recognize the cultural basis of the syndrome may escalate into a battle of wills between teacher and student with the result that the student may ultimately feel misunderstood and drop out of school. Schools are then blamed for failing to recognize such culturally based patterns. Some researchers would encourage cultural sensitivity courses for teachers. Although courses aiming to promote cross-cultural sensitivity and understanding should be encouraged, there is no evidence that Hispanic teachers have better results with Hispanic students than do White teachers.

Other exponents of this tradition emphasize that Hispanic values and worldviews prevent students from successfully manipulating the symbols required for school excellence in a White middle-class environment, in part because of fundamental incompatibilities between Hispanic and Anglo-Saxon cultures. Zintz, for example, states that Mexican American cultural tradition devalues formal education for girls. He argues that whereas success in the Anglo-Saxon world is conceived in terms of acquiring material wealth, for Mexican Americans it is framed in terms of interpersonal relations, or *amistades*. He further argues that whereas time is a precious commodity for Whites ("time is money"), the Hispanic attitude toward time is characterized by the *mañana* syndrome. The idea that time can be wasted is totally foreign and irrelevant to Hispanics. According to Zintz's logic, Hispanics have a hard time following schedules, keeping appointments, and the like, all of which would presumably have a negative effect on their schooling. Zintz argues that the Hispanic worldview is essentially fatalistic, organized around the notion that man lives "under nature," in contrast to the Anglo-Saxon conviction that nature can be tamed by human will. The *que sera sera* Hispanic approach to life, he argues, fosters an almost pathological passivity and submissiveness to the status quo.

Zintz's assessment relies on placing the blame on these value orientations for the subordinate condition of Hispanics in the United States. As Carter and Segura point out, it may turn out that fatalism itself, rather than being the cause for Hispanic educational and economic marginality, may be "a cultural adaptation to powerlessness" (1979: 87). Is the root of the problem that Hispanic American children are culturally different and must therefore be trained to acculturate to White norms? Or is the problem that Hispanic Americans, particularly Mexican Americans, having faced economic deprivation and castelike barriers for generations, have formulated shared responses that further removed them from the educational system?

Language discontinuities between the Hispanic home and the English-speaking middle-class school system have also received systematic attention in the debate over school adaptation of ethnic minorities.* Much of this research relates in one way or another to the pioneer work of J. Gumperz and his associates on the study of sociolinguistics (see Gumperz 1981, 1982, 1983; Erickson and Mohatt 1982; McDermott 1974; Mehan 1978; Hymes 1974). According to Gumperz, communication is a complex phenomenon that includes verbal utterances, "situated meanings" (speakers' intentions), and "context" (speakers' perceptions of the social situation). In order to achieve understanding and communication, persons must also share the appropriate metacommunication cues: intonation, code switching, stress, syntax, and loudness, which are culturally determined.†

* See Amastae and Elias-Olivares 1982; Barkin et al. 1982; Fishman and Keller 1982; Carter and Segura 1979.
† See Ogbu 1982*a*; Gumperz 1981.

According to Gumperz (1983), face-to-face ethnic interactions in small settings such as the classroom often capture and re-create the inequalities that permeate the larger sociocultural atmosphere. The classroom thus represents a microcosm of the larger socioeconomic setting and perpetuates social inequality through interethnic miscommunication between the teacher and student.* John Ogbu has written that "the significance of these and other theories based on classroom studies is their elucidation of the processes or mechanisms by which school failure and school success are achieved. This knowledge is very useful in developing intervention programs (e.g., for preparation of teachers) and in encouraging cautious interpretations of quantitative studies of children's academic performance." He goes on to point out in his next paragraph, however, that

These theories cannot claim to provide general explanations of minority children's school failure or failure to learn to read. This is partly because the theories are based on research on one type of minority students, namely, *castelike minorities* (Ogbu 1978). They have yet to be applied to other minorities (e.g., immigrants) who are more successful in schools, although they have cultural and communicative backgrounds different from those of their public school teachers. [Ogbu 1982*a*: 290]

Other scholars have also expressed reservations about a purely linguistic approach to the problem of minority nonlearning. De Vos, for example, has written:

Recently there has been the espousal of linguistic theories to explain differential learning in the American classroom. The reasoning of those talking about language disadvantage, even what they term "cultural disadvantage," is, I believe, somewhat simplistic. For example, one often hears that the basic reason why Mexican Americans or black children do not learn well in American schools is that they use a different or a separate language at home. Why is it that this disadvantage is overcome by some children with equally different cultural backgrounds? Why is it that the so-called Nisei children of Japanese immigrants of the 1930's and after, did quite well in schools, despite the poor linguistic competence of their parents and their own evident difficulty with English on achievement tests administered to them . . . ? I believe that the

---

* For an analysis of classroom micropolitics and its consequences for learning and nonlearning among Hispanics, see Suarez-Orozco 1987*a*.

disadvantage of speaking a foreign language at home is secondary to the social and personal meanings attached to learning an alien tongue. [De Vos 1980: 114]

Minority Status and Schooling

In considering schooling issues among minority youths, I examine both the sociological and the psychological variables mediating human intrapsychic adjustment and behavioral adaptation. Next, I juxtapose various ideas adduced by anthropologists John Ogbu and George De Vos to establish a dual, psychosocial perspective on the problem of minority schooling. Ogbu (1974, 1978, 1981, 1982b) has advocated a cultural ecological model for understanding the relationships between minority status and schooling problems in plural societies, arguing that poor school performance is a syndrome usually associated with what he calls castelike minorities. According to his model, the school system is linked strongly to wider sociohistorical factors such as the economic opportunity structure and political forces (see Ogbu 1978: 15–42). It follows that any model that concerns itself exclusively with studying microscopic classroom processes, at the expense of ignoring the larger forces, is regarded with a certain suspicion. Ogbu's aim is, in fact, to "integrate economic, political, cognitive, and behavioral structures into a single frame of analysis" (Ogbu 1982: 280). A number of key concepts, such as "castelike status," "system of status mobility" (see also LeVine 1967), the "job ceiling," and "affective dissonance" (see also De Vos 1978) and others are introduced to help explain the persistent educational problems facing certain minorities in plural societies.

For heuristic purposes, Ogbu calls castelike minorities those groups in the United States that were originally incorporated into the society against their will: for example, Blacks through slavery, Mexican Americans through the American colonization of the Southwest territories, Puerto Ricans following the American colonial takeover from Spain, and the American Indians (Ogbu 1978: 11–42, 217–38). In his opinion, not only were these groups incorporated into a new social order against their will, but historically they were relegated by virtue of birth to the lower niches in the economic opportunity structure, where education and academic effort were historically irrelevant to their social reality. Traditionally, castelike minorities are exploited for cheap labor and are thereby excluded from the more desirable occupational niches. They face a job ceiling above which they cannot rise, regardless of talent, motivation, or achievement (see Ogbu 1978: 28–29). Since they cannot compete for certain jobs as individuals because of their ascribed ethnic status, their education and their "folk system of social mobility"—their agenda for getting ahead—historically had no correlation. For these minorities occupation was determined more by birth than by educational effort.

Educational investment does not offer castelike minorities the same rewards in the labor market that it does to the majority population. In 1977, for example, Hispanic high school graduates in the United States had a higher unemployment rate than their White counterparts. Moreover, the statistical record shows that whereas Hispanic youths had higher average unemployment rates than White youths, Hispanic school dropouts had a higher employment rate than White dropouts (Brown et al. 1980: 226–27, 229). The pressure to work was a key factor in the decision to drop out of school in the first place, just as it was among some new arrivals from Central America. At all levels of educational attainment (less than eight years, eight years, one to three years of high school, four years of high school, one to three years of college, four years of college or more), "the unemployment rate for Hispanics exceeded that for Whites," and likewise, among those employed, "at each educational level Hispanic men earned less than White men" (Brown et al. 1980: 253).

It is important to note that the gap between educational attainment and posteducational economic rewards is wider for those Hispanics with a long history of subordination vis-à-vis the majority White population—that is, wider for Puerto Rican Americans and Mexican Americans than for the other Hispanics of Central and South American origin (Brown et al. 1980: 246–47) and for Cuban Americans. Goho and Smith (1973), in comparing earning patterns among White Americans and Mexican Americans with respect to the relative influence of educational attainment, found that Mexican American college graduates earned less than White Americans with the same level of educational attainment. Furthermore, Mexican Americans with one to three years of college earned, on average, only 10 percent more than

White high-school graduates. Some scholars, in fact, have argued that there is a "schooling penalty" against castelike minorities (see Blair 1971, 1972; reviewed in Ogbu 1978: 233–34). As Ogbu summarizes:

[Blair] compared the benefits measured by wages, received by Anglo-Americans and Mexican-Americans of the same levels of education. He compared two paired groups of Mexican-Americans and Anglo-Americans based on areas of residence. One pair lived in predominantly Mexican-American barrios, and the other pair lived outside the barrios. In each case, Blair found that the Mexican-American group earned lower wages than the Anglo-American group, when the two groups had the same level of education. Among those living in the barrios, the Anglo-Americans earned $880 more per year than Mexican-Americans with the same level of education; among those living outside the barrios, the Anglo-Americans earned $1713 more. Blair calls the wage differential a "schooling penalty" against the Mexican-American.

Blair's research further suggests that the schooling penalty against Mexican Americans increases as they move up in educational attainment. That is, the earnings gap between White Americans and Mexican Americans is greater when both are college graduates than when both groups drop out of school. The sad paradox is that Mexican Americans only come close to parity at the lower end of the opportunity structure. In short, among castelike minorities education has yet to emerge as the avenue to achieving parity in the posteducational world. A consequence of this pattern is that castelike minorities do not usually view education as a viable system of status mobility (see Ogbu and Matute-Bianchi 1986; Matute-Bianchi 1985).

According to this model, the high-dropout patterns and other measurements of educational failure among castelike minorities such as Blacks, Mexican Americans, mainland Puerto Ricans, and American Indians are a cultural-ecological adaptation to limited posteducational opportunities. The cold question remains: Why should a Mexican American youth invest time and struggle through school and college if at the end, on average, he will likely earn only 10 percent more than if he had graduated only from high school? The economic factors linking schooling and the labor market do not add up for castelike minorities the way they do for the majority population.

Finally, Ogbu and his associates concur with De Vos (1984)

that castelike minorities also face systematic forms of "expressive exploitation" or "depreciation" by the majority population. For example, these minorities are commonly viewed by the majority population as innately intellectually inferior, lazy, less capable of self-regulation, and therefore incapable of fully sharing in the amenities of life in the affluent society.* These factors, as we shall see, serve to dissuade castelike minorities from believing that education is an investment in their future.

The work in psychological anthropology by George De Vos and his associates (see De Vos 1978, 1980, 1982, 1983*b*, 1984; Wagatsuma and De Vos 1984; De Vos and Suarez-Orozco 1987) illuminates the complex psychosocial consequences of prolonged minority exploitation and disparagement in plural societies such as the United States and Japan. Based upon extended fieldwork among minorities in both countries, De Vos has constructed a model of human psychological functioning that may heuristically be conceived as analogous to the operations of the biological cell. According to this model, three elemental functions govern the development of the human ego: (1) intake, (2) exclusion, or boundary protection, and (3) expulsion. These mechanisms are universal and, in their most primitive forms, have been called introjection, denial, and projection. They "survive" in mature and well-functioning adults: intake, for example, develops into a mature capacity for human empathy; exclusion facilitates concentration in thought; and expulsion leads to a human capacity to objectify thinking (see De Vos 1980: 101–24).

Through these mechanisms the human ego selectively regulates the inflow of experience. Toxic stimuli are prevented from permeating the organism. A fear of potential toxicity from the environment leads to excessive rigidification of the protecting membrane. Learning in the classroom, as indeed in any other context, depends on the equilibratory functioning of this mechanism. In Piagetian terms (Piaget 1930; Piaget and Inhelder 1969), to achieve the creative tension between the accommodative and the assimilative processes required for learning, the inflow-outflow mechanism must not rigidify. De Vos (1984) notes that patterns of instrumental and expressive exploitation lead to

* For an analysis of White popular images of Mexican Americans, see Cortes 1985.

forms of ego rigidification and the emergence of non-learning strategies among minority students (see De Vos 1978, 1980). Continuous defense against a perceived danger in the encompassing environment eventually leads to an exclusionary rigidification of the ego, specifically sensitive to probing from the dominant world of the majority. De Vos calls this process "selective permeability" (1978: 7–24). That is, certain social stimuli that would endanger one's guarded self will not be allowed to penetrate and cause accommodative changes within. Or, as teachers in the inner city would put it, the students "just can't learn."

According to this model, the continuous depreciation historically faced by Blacks and Mexican Americans in the United States has had specific psychosocial consequences for classroom behavior, which in turn have been vigorously reinforced by peer-group sanctionings. In an atmosphere of interethnic tension, mutual distrust, resentment, and peer-group sanctioning, such as prevails in the inner-city classroom, castelike minority students find it hard to learn. De Vos suggests that they may in fact be practicing "defensive non-learning" (De Vos 1978: 7–24). In these contexts the formal schooling system, run by Whites or with an agenda set by Whites, becomes a psychological threat to the student's sense of ethnic identity and belonging. Castelike minority students may feel that success in school requires behaviors and strategies that they associate with the "Anglo" way of being. And "Anglos" are often viewed as the oppressors, who keep the group down and use the educational system to maintain the inequalities of the status quo (see Matute-Bianchi 1985; Ogbu and Matute-Bianchi 1986).

The perception of the peer group as a powerful mediator emerging between school and home must be examined. Current scholarship in anthropology and education tends to emphasize the effect of home/school discontinuities on the schooling of minority students, but it has generally neglected to consider how peer-group dynamics affect their schooling experience. As a socialization agent the peer group has been noted to punish severely behavior that appears to threaten the sense of group cohesion. For example, there are reports that certain Black youth in schools speak "standard" English only at the risk of censure by their peers for "acting White," or being "fake." Research among Black students in the Washington, D.C., area indicates that successful Blacks underplay, minimize, or even hide their scholastic success in order to avoid the wrath of their peer groups (Fordham and Ogbu 1986: 176–206). Similarly, successful Mexican American youngsters from East Los Angeles reported to me that during their high school years they were teased and otherwise ridiculed by their peers for studying too hard. One young man recalled that his friends used to call him, not without sarcasm, "Mr. Engineer," because he was such a good student in mathematics. When the friends of another youth heard that he was going away to college, they jibed, "You think you're better than we are, don't you?" In this context, to do well in school may be defined by the peer group as the wish to act White, or be "Anglo," and to reject or turn away from one's own ethnic group.

It may then be psychologically unacceptable for many castelike minority students, who come to define themselves in opposition to the dominant world of the Whites or Anglos (Ogbu and Matute-Bianchi 1986; Fordham and Ogbu 1986), to behave in the manner required to succeed in school. De Vos writes: "In situations of cultural pluralism, class differentiation, or strongly defined sex roles, certain forms of comportment are, in a sense, not to be entertained without emotional as well as cognitive dissonance" (De Vos 1980: 115). Among certain youth, success in school may induce a state of "affective dissonance" when it is equated with a wish to "act Anglo" and leave one's ethnic group behind. In that instance a minority individual may have to choose between being a proud member of his or her ethnic group or a success story in the Anglo-Saxon idiom. This seems to be the point of Richard Rodriguez's (1982) tale. A graduate of Stanford and Berkeley and a postgraduate fellow at a prestigious British institution, Rodriguez "just can't" go back to his humble Sacramento barrio to be with his working-class parents. A severe sense of alienation from his family, particularly his father, overwhelms him. Rodriguez resolves this dissonant state by leaving his group behind in his journey through the affluent society—at great emotional cost. His almost studied alienation from his family, however, limits the applications his case may have to the Mexican American experience at large.

The psychosocial approach seems to explain the much-discussed issue of alienation from school among some Hispanics, principally Mexican Americans and Puerto Rican students (see Romo 1984; HPDP 1984). Recent scholarly research also suggests that De Vos's generalizations are applicable to key issues facing Mexican Americans in schools.* Scholars argue that many Mexican American students view and experience the schooling system as a tool used by the majority culture to maintain the inequality of the status quo. Some Mexican American informants appear to show a severe distrust of educational institutions. Tests seem to be viewed by some students and parents not as legitimate tools to evaluate learning patterns, but as instruments for maintaining students at lower levels. Romo found a pattern of more severe alienation from school among Chicano families in Texas; she concluded that compared with immigrant Mexicans, "Chicano parents expressed the most alienation from the schools" (1984: 646).

Immigrants and Schools

A number of scholars have been concerned recently with the problematic issue of variability in minority status and school functioning (Gibson 1987, in press; Ogbu 1982*b*, 1985; Ogbu and Matute-Bianchi 1986; Suarez-Orozco 1986, 1987*a*, 1988). In the simplest terms, these scholars have been asking, in Ogbu's words, "*why some minority groups, why some language minorities do quite well in school despite cultural and language barriers*" (Ogbu and Matute-Bianchi 1986: 74; their emphasis; see also Ogbu 1984, 1985). In fact, not all minorities do poorly in school. Research suggests that many immigrant minorities who must struggle with the upheaval of migration and resettlement, as well as with language, discontinuities in communication, limited economic resources, and social barriers, eventually overcome hardships and do quite well in school in the host society. Why then are many immigrant minorities capable of crossing cultural boundaries and eventually doing well in school, whereas large proportions of castelike minorities continue to fail?

Research among immigrant groups has shown that they can learn the new language and eventually do well in school, apparently without experiencing "affective dissonance," without

* See Ogbu and Matute-Bianchi 1986: 111–42; Matute-Bianchi 1985; HPDP 1984; Romo 1984; Fernandez and Marenco 1980.

having to forfeit a sense of their ethnicity. The Japanese Americans, the Korean Americans, and the Punjabi Sikhs in California are examples of immigrant minorities that succeeded in American schools (De Vos 1983a: 25–71; Gibson 1983, 1987, in press), perhaps contrary to the predictions of certain models.

Certain key features differentiate immigrants from castelike minorities. In the United States, whereas the latter were incorporated into the society against their will and were subsequently relegated to the lower sectors of the opportunity structure, immigrant minorities generally chose, more or less freely, to leave their country of origin to enter a new socioeconomic order. In this sense, immigrants and castelike minorities differ in their earlier experiences with the encompassing majority population.

In addition, immigrants have been called "birds of passage" because they commonly anticipate that they may one day return home to the old country to enjoy the fruits of their labor in a foreign land (see Piore 1979; Suarez-Orozco 1987b). In fact, the immigrant dream of success is more often about returning home than about staying on to acculturate or to succeed economically in the host society. The prospect of a return may help many individuals to endure discrimination and hardship in the host society. Castelike minorities, however—utopian intellectual movements notwithstanding—do not generally entertain concrete plans or proposals for going home. For Blacks and Chicanos, home is the United States,* for better or worse. Immigrants commonly view their experiences in the host land in terms of opportunity. At the outset, they usually inhabit the lower sectors of the labor market (Lieberson 1980: 308–20). Reports of Korean physicians selling vegetables in American inner cities sensationalize the point that immigrants are very willing to take low-status jobs, without necessarily sharing "the invidious definitions the dominant group attaches to their menial positions" (Ogbu 1982b: 3).

Two factors seem to alleviate the poisonous, long-term effects of the discrimination and hardships that immigrants often face. In the first place, discrimination appears to be most acute against

---

* Some Chicano intellectuals have advocated a return to Aztlan, the mythical place of Aztec origin, a golden Edenic land north of today's Mexico, i.e., somewhere in the United States (see Chavez 1984).

the first, foreign-born generation, who look and sound particularly distinct. For the American-born generation, particularly among White immigrants from Eastern, Southern, and Central Europe, the levels of discrimination became less evident as accents disappeared and names were anglicized (Lieberson 1980: 30–34). In short, as Ogbu points out, although "subject to pillory and discrimination, [immigrants] have not usually had the time to internalize the effects of discrimination [n]or have those effects become an ingrained part of their culture" (Ogbu 1982b: 3–4). This is quite different from the experience of castelike minorities, generation after generation. Second, a fundamental feature of the migrant experience is the emergence of what I term a "dual frame of reference" in the immigrants' worldview, as they resettle in a new land. They have the luxury of being able to compare their current reality with that of the life they have left behind. And regardless of how "bad off" a given group may appear to an outsider, the immigrants themselves may in fact feel better off than in the country of origin. Castelike minorities, on the other hand, have no dual frame of reference: they may view their current reality as a basic continuity in a long history of subordination vis-à-vis the majority population (see Ogbu 1978). My data suggest that this dual frame of reference helps insulate many immigrants from the discrimination they nevertheless do encounter, particularly in the inner city. Furthermore, a basic driving force common to most immigrants is the belief that hard work in the new land is certain at least to benefit their children. For many of them, the future looks bright.

Among immigrant parents from Central America in my sample, the education and future of the children was both a reason for enduring sacrifices and the greatest reward. For them as for other immigrant groups, success in the school system is in no way associated with passing, or with acting White, or with a wish to leave one's ethnic group behind. Rather, successful Central American students framed their efforts in more instrumental terms. They wished to take full advantage of educational opportunities not available at home, such as learning computers and a new language, and in general to equip themselves with skills to use back home if the family chooses to return.

A psychosocial approach that examines both the experiential

or "emic" side of adaptation to schooling and the sociohistorical and economic contexts in which the actors play their parts would predict that the immigrant students from Central America would encounter, if not fewer, then different problems than would castelike minorities such as U.S. Blacks and Mexican Americans. In general, immigrant Hispanics tend to do better in American educational settings than do either mainland Puerto Ricans or Mexican Americans.

Indeed, the immigrant population that I studied faced a number of school problems associated with what has been termed the immigrant's "primary cultural differences" from the majority population; that is, those differences between two cultural groups that existed prior to contact between them (Ogbu 1984: 3). Language is one example. Central American immigrants in the United States speak a wholly different language, Spanish. That alone creates problems in the classroom. More important is the fact that the immigrants anticipate a different form of cultural communication. According to my informants, teaching styles, particularly the way in which teachers exercise authority, are perceived differently in the two cultures. Conversely, teachers' perceptions of students and the role of parents lead to failure of communication, which in turn results in misunderstanding and conflict. For example, immigrant Hispanics thought that silence in the classroom was the sine qua non for respect, yet some White teachers cited it as evidence of "Latin passivity." In one case, the quieter the students remained, the more frustrated and angry the teacher became, which made the immigrant students yet quieter. And so on.

Furthermore, many immigrant students cannot comprehend the lack of both discipline and respect for the teacher in the inner-city classroom. When I asked the new arrivals what they liked least about their new schools, almost invariably they mentioned the insolence and disrespect of the other students toward the teachers. Vlach, in her study of families recently arrived in the United States from Guatemala, reports a similar concern: "They [the immigrant family] feel that there is too much drug-taking, loose morality, and not enough control (in the classroom) of the behavior of these [U.S.] adolescents" (1984: 64). Immigrant parents do not understand the general permissiveness in the classroom. They expect greater initiative on the part of teachers and are ready to comply with their directives.* One of the more superficial problems that came to light was the fact that immigrant students had great difficulty with multiple-choice tests, which are uncommon in Central America.

The thesis that Hispanic immigrants sometimes perform better in school than their castelike counterparts is vitiated by studies showing that U.S.-born Mexican Americans tend to do better in school than their Mexican-born peers. The figures in a recent study show that up to 70 percent of the Mexican-born Hispanics in U.S. schools may be dropping out of school, a figure much higher than that for comparable Mexican American students (see Becklund 1985: 1–3). This shocking figure says nothing about why these students are leaving school. The implications for a theory of minority status and schooling would differ depending upon the salience of reasons for leaving school. Do immigrant students leave American schools because they return to Mexico, as many doubtlessly do, perhaps to continue schooling there? Do they reluctantly give up a strong desire to study in order to join the labor force and help the family, as did some of the recent Central American immigrants? Do they leave because they realize that their legal status in the United States will not permit them to continue studying, as was the case with some of my Central American informants? Or do they share an inner conviction that schooling is irrelevant to the nature of their reality?

Before considering the Central American immigrant case, let us examine briefly certain key issues for the Mexican immigrant case. Indeed, several factors seem to discount the Mexican case as a heuristically paradigmatic immigrant minority. First, the Mexican Republic lost roughly one-third of its territory to the colonialists from the North (see Chavez 1984; Rosenbaum 1981; Weber 1973; Lopez y Rivas 1973; McWilliams 1968). For many Mexicans, including immigrants, the psychological effect of this disaster was a deep and abiding resentment (see Suarez-Orozco 1987b; see also Riding 1984). Another factor for many Mexican immigrants is that they are leaving a social system based on peonage and denigration at home, the product of Mexico's own complex colonial and postcolonial experience. In some respects,

---

* For a consideration of family-school discontinuities and their effects on interaction, see Hansen 1986.

lower-status groups in Mexico, who provide many of the immigrants, face problems similar to those encountered in more overtly castelike situations by American Blacks, Native Americans, and Mexican Americans. At the turn of the century, in an earlier cycle of immigration, the ex-serfs of Poland showed a poorer school performance than did other Eastern European migrants to the United States. Systems of denigration and educational deprivation, it appears, are usually found side-by-side with castelike rigidity of social status.

Historical conditions and close physical proximity to the United States, which encourages seasonal return-migration, have made Mexican residents aware of the continuing subordinate status of their brothers and sisters in the United States. A recent episode makes the point: when President Carter appointed a Mexican American to be the U.S. ambassador to Mexico, some members of the Mexican government were offended by the gesture. Their interpretation was that the American government was appointing a "second-class citizen" to this prestigious post (see Riding 1984). Furthermore, as Ogbu has argued, White Americans continue to treat Mexican immigrants as a castelike minority despite their immigrant status. That is, "later immigrants from Mexico moved into the social and technoeconomic climate established between local Mexican-Americans and Anglos at the time of the conquest" (Ogbu 1978: 225). More directly related to the status of some of the recent arrivals from Central America is the fact that large numbers of these immigrants reside in the United States without the legal documentation required to live, work, and study in this country.* That may explain in part why undocumented immigrants, who appear eager to offer schooling to their children, seem unable nevertheless to make effective use of the American educational system.

According to the theoretical model for exploring the psychosocial contexts of learning and non-learning among minority students, the problems facing castelike minorities, such as Mexican Americans and Puerto Rican Americans, are distinct from those facing such immigrant minorities as Korean Americans or

---

* See Lewis 1980; for discussions of undocumented aliens in the United States, see Cornelius 1982; Cross and Sandos 1981; Portes 1978; Monge et al. 1977; Tylor 1976; Samora 1971.

Central Americans. They are framed in a cultural-ecological and psychological framework that examines the effect on schooling of (1) a "job-ceiling" in the posteducational opportunity structure; (2) a continuous pattern of expressive and instrumental exploitation; and (3) the significant psychological and behavioral responses to inequality over generations that also prevent school success.

Immigrants, on the other hand, enter a new social order, presumably with the intention of bettering their lot. In the process of resettlement, the emergence of an immigrant ethic (see Chapter 5) may insulate many of them from the depreciation and hardships they may endure in the host society. Central American immigrants should, according to this model, experience specific school problems that relate to their primary cultural differences from the majority population. A further, major issue facing many recent Central American immigrants is that many do not possess the required documentation to study, work, or even live in the United States. Unlike "formal" immigrants who usually settle with some sort of permanent legal right to work and study in the host society (see Lieberson 1980: 98–99), the undocumented Central American immigrants cannot be considered a paradigmatic population representing a classic immigrant adaptation to schooling. Their marginal legal status directly interferes with their school functioning.

In other respects the Central Americans do fit the more ordinary American immigrant pattern. They have come to the United States of their own will. Although some were escaping politically inspired violence, prevailing U.S. attitudes prevent their classification as political refugees. Yet, the war and economic strife that they escaped has affected, and even obstructed, their subsequent adaptation to U.S. schools. A dream to achieve a better tomorrow through self-sacrifice has enabled many of the recent arrivals, parents and children alike, to endure marginality (legal, economic, linguistic, etc.) and to move toward attempts to succeed despite the unfavorable climate of the American inner city. It is all the more remarkable how they are attempting to overcome the chaotic conditions they encounter in the inner city—gang warfare, drugs, burned-out teachers, hostile counselors, overcrowded and understaffed classrooms, mediocre pedagogical programs, tracking into classes of dubious benefit, pressures to help the family economically, as well as the disruptive effect of the continuing wars on family members left behind. Many of these new arrivals in my sample went on to become good students, to graduate, and in some cases to enter prestigious colleges.

THREE

Escape to Freedom: Political Violence and Economic Scarcity in Central America

THE EXPERIENCE OF recent Central American immigrants appears to be related to more ordinary patterns of immigrant settlement. Most of my informants had left their homeland in a context of increasing political violence and economic scarcity in order to establish themselves more advantageously in the United States. Unlike typical immigrants, however, many of these Central Americans lacked the legal documentation required for residence in the United States. It will be relevant to their story to analyze how my informants constructed, albeit retrospectively, a key aspect of their migrant experience: their reasons for leaving Central America and the resultant set of specific ongoing interpersonal concerns.

This study was not intended to explore whether recent arrivals from Central America are technically refugees or economic migrants. I do not have the kind of data required for evaluating this question in a systematic and meaningful manner and can therefore not contribute to this argument (see Mohn 1983). I call the new arrivals "immigrants," using the term in its widest sense to refer to those moving to a new country or region in order to settle there, more or less permanently. It is also not my purpose to discuss the sanctuary movement in the United States and its efforts to shelter and give voice to the voiceless from Central America (see Golden and McConnell 1986). As the research progressed, I became aware that current issues in the lives of my informants were intimately related to the continuing situation at home. They themselves had escaped physically, but not psychologically. They repeatedly referred to what was happening at the time they left Central America, as well as to what was going on at "home" at the time of the research. Over 60 percent of them had one or more members of their nuclear family still residing in war-torn Central America (see Table 6.2).

In late 1984, when rumors of a possible U.S. invasion of Nicaragua permeated the American press, and gossip about developments there was rampant among the Nicaraguans in the inner city barrios, Amadeo was anxious about the fate of his parents and older sister still in Managua. They had sent him out of the country less than a year earlier, to escape the military draft. Indeed, there have been reports of a recent exodus of Nicaraguan youths into Costa Rica and other countries, as 15-year-olds-and-above became targets of Sandinista army recruiting tactics. Amadeo had settled down with an aunt and uncle in the United States, but he was emotionally very much preoccupied with developments at home. During those tense weeks in late 1984, Amadeo seemed restless. He was not sleeping well at night, and he appeared increasingly impatient with seemingly pointless routines at school. Yet he was determined to stay on and graduate.

It was at this point that Amadeo told me he had begun working at night, principally to "save money to help get her [his sister] out of Nicaragua." She was in hiding, somewhere in Managua, to avoid the military draft, which had been extended to women. He would save enough money so she could bribe her way out, he said. These issues alerted me to the emergence of a specific motivational pattern: these youths shared a keen sense of responsibility to those who, one way or another, had sacrificed their own safety to allow someone else to flee to the United States.

All of my informants had left Central America within five years prior to the beginning of my research. What they told me informally and in formal interviews recalls some of the recent findings in the field of Central American studies. In this context, I shall analyze a key legacy of remembrances of things past: the psychological consequences of terror, as captured in the Thematic Apperception Test (TAT), from which torture and assassination emerge as continuing concerns plaguing many who had escaped the Central American nightmare but still dreamed of it in the new setting.

"La Situación": Reflections on Political Terror and Economic Scarcity

Without exception, the informants reported having left Central America—El Salvador, Nicaragua, Guatemala—*por la situación*. They used these simple words to refer to a nightmarish world of war, disappearances, systematic torture, random killings, bodies in the streets with political messages carved in the flesh, kidnappings, forced recruitment into wars foreign to their hearts, and economic scarcity. Political terror has again become the idiom for social consensus in Central American history. The numbers of politically motivated killings appear meaningless when checked against the desperate faces of the survivors: "By late October 1983, there were at least 40,000 dead, and counting, in El Salvador; 10,000 to 20,000—one could only guess—in Guatemala; 40,000 in Nicaragua during the rebellion against Somoza, and another 1,000 since the United States began fighting its proxy war there" (Buckley 1984: 332).

It is not my intent to compile a systematic treatment of recent developments in Central America.* Rather, I propose to intertwine certain key issues found in the literature with some of the "emic," or personal, reasons given by the informants for leaving home. The overriding concern among the youth I worked with was that many of their loved ones remained in an eerie scenario of collective fear, deprivation, and death. This fact has created unique interpersonal concerns among the immigrant youth. The very *situación* my informants were personally escaping has begun to gain systematic attention in both the scholarly and the popular literatures.†

* For overviews, see Barry and Preusch 1986; Kempton 1986; Perera 1986; Chomsky 1985; LaFeber 1984; Segesvary 1984; Womack 1983; Diskin 1983; Torres-Rivas 1983; Montgomery 1982; Baloyra 1982; Quiroz 1982; McColm 1982; Anderson 1982, 1970; West and Augelli 1976; Adams 1970; Nash 1967; Brigham 1964.

† See Dickey 1987; Brown 1985; Diskin 1985, 1983; Earle 1985; Joseph and Wells 1985; Buckley 1984; LaFeber 1984; Didion 1983; Montgomery 1982.

The index of terror is indeed eerie. In El Salvador, Montgomery notes that "more than 30,000 Salvadoreans had died [i.e., been killed] since October 15, 1979" (1982: 191), out of a population of 5.1 million. Brown, writing more recently, notes:

More than 40,000 civilian noncombatants killed—murdered by government forces and "death squads" allied to them; another 3,000 disappeared; 750,000 or so (15 percent of the population) refugees beyond its border; 500,000 or so (another 10 percent of the population) homeless or "displaced" within its borders. Those are a few of the more or less familiar statistics reflecting the consequences of political violence in El Salvador, the geographically tiniest country in the landmass of the Americas. [Brown 1985: 115]

These figures seem all the more grotesque when we consider that El Salvador is a country of 8,236 square miles, about the size of Massachusetts. The genesis of these revolutionary developments in Central America, in the opinion of experts in the field, is the legacy of indecent inequality established under Spanish colonial rule and later solidified by a subsequent dependency on the United States (LaFeber 1984: 19–83; Torres-Rivas 1983: 2–33; Montgomery 1982: 33–53).*

With about 595 persons per square mile, El Salvador is the most densely populated nation in Central America. Its population growth rate of about 3.5 percent per year is one of the highest in the world. A poor country, El Salvador's economy depends heavily on agriculture, particularly coffee exports, and on American aid.† The average per capita income for all Salvadoreans is about U.S. $680 per year (LaFeber 1984: 10). The majority of the people are mestizos (some 89 percent); Indians (about 10 percent) and Caucasians (about 1 percent) are numerical minorities. The Salvadoreans are predominantly Roman Catholics, but active Protestant groups also exist in the country. Catholic priests, endorsing liberation theology, began to organize peasants actively in the 1970's.

The Catholic Church, through its *comunidades de base* or popular church communities, expedited the organizing with a theology that brought

---

* For considerations of dependency, development, and debt in Latin America, see Kim and Ruccio 1985; Cardoso and Faletto 1979.

† About 20 percent of El Salvador's 1984 GDP was from coffee. In 1984, El Salvador received $329.3 million in U.S. economic aid (see USDS 1985).

dignity to the *campesinos*. They began thinking of themselves as children of God, worthy of the right to life. They began asking why they should not occupy and use, or try to rent or buy, land left vacant by wealthy landlords. Why should weeds grow on private property while their children starved? [Golden and McConnell 1986: 18]

In 1980, the infamous "death squad" assassinations of four U.S. Maryknoll Sister missionaries and of Archbishop Oscar Romero of San Salvador indicated just how the security forces intended to deal with the church's attempts at defining its role in the unfolding conflict. Also, the assassinations made the U.S. public conscious, perhaps for the first time, of the brutal reality unfolding in Central America.

Fifty percent of the Salvadorean work force labors in agriculture, 22 percent in industry, and 27 percent in the service sector. Salvadoreans speak Spanish, although there are some Nahuatl speakers as well. Known in Central American folklore as the "Germans of Central America" for their industriousness, "many Salvadoreans historically have had to emigrate to survive" (LaFeber 1984: 10).

Legal immigration from El Salvador to the United States has been on the rise in the last three decades: 5,895 in 1951–60; 14,992 in 1961–70; 34,436 in 1971–80; and 32,666 from 1980 to 1984 (SYB 1984: 5). This emigration must be seen, in part, in the context of a patterned resource competition between different sectors of the social structure: a fierce competition for land between the rural poor and the large landowners excludes the peasants from "more than 60 percent of the nation's flattest and most fertile land" (Durham 1979: 169–70).* In fact, about 60 percent of the best Salvadorean soil continues to be in the hands of a small oligarchy known as the "fourteen families," with the consequence that the Salvadoreans "are among the world's five worst-fed populations" (LaFeber 1984: 10). Indeed, Durham reports that "80 percent of the children under five years of age in El Salvador suffer from identifiable malnutrition (i.e., their weight-for-age ratio is more than 10 percent below normal). Nearly half of these (127,000 of 268,000) are estimated to show signs of mod-

---

* For an analysis of how resource competition and Salvadorean migration to Honduras influenced the outbreak of the so-called soccer war of 1969, see Durham 1979.

erate to severe malnutrition (more than 25 percent below normal weight for age)" (1979: 7). The infant mortality rate is about 71 per thousand (vs. 13.8 in the United States). In 1970, 79.2 percent of the rural population and 20.8 percent of the urban population were illiterate (Torres-Rivas 1984: 28).

LeFeber estimates that

> Since the revolution accelerated in the late seventies, one-tenth of the population, or about 300,000 people, have entered the United States illegally for refuge. They had reasons other than economic for doing so: during 1980 and 1981 the military and right-wing terrorists killed approximately 30,000 civilians to stop spreading revolution. Such a blood bath (equivalent of killing more than two million of the U.S. population) is not new; fifty years earlier, the military killed a similar number of peasants for similar reasons. [1984: 10; see also Sheehan 1986: 25–30; for a consideration of the earlier killings or *matanza*, see Anderson 1970]

The exact number of Salvadoreans uprooted in the context of the escalating terror is still debated. The United Nations High Commissioner for Refugees indicated that over 500,000 Salvadoreans had fled their homeland since the latest wave of terror began in 1979 (Mohn 1983: 42). Others estimate that closer to 750,000 people may have fled (Brown 1985: 135), and recent reports indicate that as many as one million Salvadoreans may have left the country (Aguayo 1986: 31–32).

Of course, not all Salvadorean refugees reside in the United States. They are scattered all the way from Canada to Panama, and there are thousands in refugee camps in Honduras. Also, as many as 150,000 Salvadorean refugees are in Mexico (Aguayo 1986: 31), and possibly as many as 350,000 in other Central American nations (Cuadernos de Tercer Mundo 1984: 52–54). The Central American Refugee Committee [CRECEN] estimates that over 500,000 Salvadoreans now make the United States their place of residence (CRECEN 1985). El Salvador's president, José Napoleón Duarte, was quoted more recently as saying that "some 400,000 to 600,000 Salvadoreans have entered the United States illegally since January 1982" (Pear 1987: 1–8).

These figures are at best only tentative; since large numbers of new arrivals are in the United States without the required documentation (see Flinn 1985), it is hard to establish a reliable count.

CRECEN estimates that of about 30,000 Salvadoreans who applied for political asylum in the United States from 1980 until 1985, just under 3 percent were approved (CRECEN 1985). Similarly, Golden and McConnell report that "of fifty-five hundred requests by Salvadoreans for political asylum in fiscal year 1980–81 only two were granted" (1986: 42). According to Immigration and Naturalization Service figures, in fiscal 1984, 13,045 Salvadorean applications for asylum were denied, about one-third of all denials for applicants from some 120 different countries; and only 503 were granted (SYB 1984: 77). For this very reason some of the new arrivals escaping El Salvador do not bother to apply for political asylum. One informant reported, in fact, that as many as 30,000 Salvadoreans may have been deported from the United States back to El Salvador since 1980. In fiscal 1984, 18,957 aliens from El Salvador were identified as deportable, but in fact 2,619 of them were deported (SYB 1984: 211). During fiscal 1984 and the first seven months of fiscal 1985, the San Diego sector of the United States Border Patrol alone arrested 6,152 Salvadoreans entering the country without the required documentation (Flinn 1985), the largest group of aliens "other than Mexican" arrested in that period of time.

Guatemala has a population of 8,335,000 people (July 1985), living in a territory about the size of the state of Tennessee (42,000 square miles). It has a high average rate of population growth of 3.1 percent. Its economy depends heavily on agriculture, specifically coffee, banana, and cotton exports. Fifty-seven percent of the total Guatemalan work force labors in agriculture; 14 percent in manufacturing; the remaining work in services, commerce, construction, and so forth. The unemployment rate in Guatemala fluctuates around 33 percent. A devastating earthquake in 1976 killed over 20,000 people, injured thousands more, and destroyed much of the rural highland landscape, leaving thousands homeless (USDS 1984).

Spanish is the dominant language, but more than 40 percent of the population speak Indian languages, such as Quiche, Cakchiquel, or Kekchi. Guatemalans are predominantly Roman Catholic, yet Protestant and traditional Mayan religions are also part of the sociocultural framework. When Guatemalan Catholic priests, like their Salvadorean brothers, attempted to organize peasants and Indians demanding certain basic rights, they too were dealt with swiftly and brutally, a part of a larger counterinsurgency campaign (see Brown 1985: 180–294).

Although Guatemala is economically the most powerful nation in the Central American region, half the population average only $81 in income per year (LaFeber 1984: 8). In 1980 the legal minimum wage, according to Davis (1983: 165), was $1.12 per day. Shelton Davis reports that "most of the studies by rural sociologists that discuss the social and economic significance of the pattern of *latifundio-minifundio* land tenure in Guatemala mention the fact that 2 percent of the farmers own more than 53 percent of the cultivable land, while another 77 percent of the farmers do not have enough land to subsist" (1983: 159). The infant mortality rate in Guatemala is 79 per thousand, slightly higher than in El Salvador (USDS 1984: 1). In the early 1970's the unemployment rate in the countryside was about 42 percent (Davis 1983: 161). Throughout the 1960's and 1970's, 81.9 percent of Guatemala's rural population and 18.1 percent of its urban population were illiterate (Torres-Rivas 1983: 28).

According to both LaFeber (1984: 8–9) and Davis (1983: 161–63), by the 1970's the poor landless, mostly Maya Indians, began to organize into revolutionary units demanding a greater share of the nation's wealth. Following Eric Wolf (1969), Davis interprets developments in the Guatemalan countryside as a "modern peasant war" (1984: 156–71). The revolts were crushed by a brutal military counterinsurgency campaign "aimed at physically and psychologically terrorizing the rural population" (Davis 1984: 166; see also Perera 1986: 39–43; Earle 1985). The body count of the recent Guatemalan blood bath varies from about 30,000 killed between 1970 and 1984 (Davis 1984: 156) to a high of 80,000 political deaths (estimate by Torres-Rivas 1983: 29). A culture of terror establishing social consensus through violence and intimidation has flourished. "In contemporary Guatemala, political violence has become more than merely commonplace. Under a series of army-dominated regimes that have ruled Guatemala since 1954, political terror has firmly established itself as the principal means of governance" (Brown 1985: 1980). The National Bishops' Conference reported that

Violence has taken possession of Guatemala. . . . [We decry] the irrational use of torture; massacres of entire families and groups, above all Indians and *campesinos,* including children, pregnant women, and old people; massive displacement of families and segments of the population seeking security and losing their homes and possessions, giving rise to refugees abroad who have to endure the most inhuman levels of misery and uncertainty. [Brown 1985: 182]

As a consequence of the arguably genocidal campaign to crush the peasant revolt, the Roman Catholic Bishops' Conference of Guatemala estimated that "as many as one million Guatemalans may be refugees." The U.S. State Department's estimates are more conservative, about 250,000 Guatemalans displaced in the context of the war (Mohn 1983: 42). These figures too are probably not reliable. We should also not assume that all uprooted Guatemalans now reside in the United States: Mexican estimates indicate that some 46,000 Guatemalans have been given refuge in Mexico (Van Praag 1986: 20–22).

More than 220,000 recent arrivals from Guatemala are now residing in the United States, according to CRECEN estimates (1985); and of all Guatemalans applying for political asylum since 1980, only 0.3 percent had been approved. In fiscal year 1984, some 4,956 deportable aliens from Guatemala were identified by the Immigration and Naturalization Service. According to U.S. border patrol figures, Guatemalans were the second largest group of aliens "other than Mexican" arrested by the San Diego sector, and 851 Guatemalan nationals were deported from the United States (SYB 1984: 189, 211). Legal immigration from Guatemala to the United States has also been on the rise in the past decades: in 1951–60, 4,663 Guatemalans immigrated to the United States with proper documentation; 15,883 in 1961–70; 25,882 in 1971–80; and 15,606 in 1981–84 (SYB 1984: 5).

Nicaragua, with about 3 million people (July 1985), is the least densely populated nation in Central America and the largest in area (57,000 square miles, about the size of Iowa). Its annual rate of population growth is 3.5 percent. Nicaragua's economy depends primarily on agriculture, mostly cotton, coffee, sugar, and timber exports (LaFeber 1984: 11). Some 40 percent of the work force labors in agriculture, 36 percent in the service sector; the rest work in industry, construction, and other occupations.

There is a 25 percent unemployment rate. In 1984, the average annual per capita income in Nicaragua was $1,132.

Nicaraguans are predominantly Roman Catholic (95 percent of the population). Ethnically, 69 percent of the population is mestizo, 17 percent White, 9 percent Black, and 5 percent Indian. Although Spanish is the official language, both English and Indian languages are spoken, particularly on the Nicaraguan Atlantic coast.

By the nineteenth century U.S. interests became increasingly aware of the strategic importance of the Nicaraguan Rift, the natural passageway across the Rivas Isthmus, connecting the Caribbean Sea and the Pacific Ocean. Indeed, "perhaps more than any other Central American country, Panama excepted, Nicaragua has felt the direct influence of the United States in its politics and economy" (West and Augelli 1976: 438).

From 1934 until 1979 Nicaragua was ruled by the U.S.-backed Somoza dynasty. Following a series of U.S. military occupations of Nicaragua throughout the 1910's and 1920's and into the early 1930's, General Anastasio Somoza, "a hustler, a heavy charmer, and a real killer," was installed as the first head of what would become a series of legendary brutal governments (Womack 1983: xv). In a continent with a long history of dictatorships, he won the dubious distinction of heading "the longest, most corrupt dictatorship in Latin America" (Barry and Preusch 1986: 272). Franklin D. Roosevelt made his own diagnosis of Somoza: "He is a sonofabitch, but he's ours" (Womack 1983: xv).

LaFeber has estimated that at a time when about 200,000 peasants had no land, the Somoza clan "seized most of the wealth, including a land area equal to the size of Massachusetts" (1984: 11). In July 1979, after two decades of guerrilla warfare against Somoza's army (the U.S.-trained National Guard), the Frente Sandinista ousted the Somozas and eventually installed a nine-member national directorate of the Sandinista National Front. The Reagan administration, arguing that the leftist Sandinistas were a threat to the security of the region, began a notorious campaign to remove them from power.* Nicaragua's illiteracy rate prior to the Sandinista takeover was between 60 and 70 per-

---

* For a journalistic account of the U.S.-backed *Contra* effort to overthrow the Sandinistas, see Dickey 1987.

cent (LaFeber 1984: 11), which the Sandinistas reduced to about 13 percent (Fagan 1983: 147).

During the bloody war to overthrow Somoza, an estimated 40,000 Nicaraguans were killed (see Buckley 1984: 332; LaFeber 1984: 226–42), and some 200,000 Nicaraguans left their country in search of refuge in Mexico, other Central American nations, and the United States (Quezada 1985: 37). Since the Sandinista takeover in 1979, thousands more have died in the U.S.-backed contra war (Dickey 1987; Kempton 1986: 5–11; Buckley 1984: 332). The San Diego sector of the U.S. border patrol reported capturing only 723 Nicaraguans during fiscal year 1984 and into the first seven months of fiscal 1985. That figure would indicate that significantly fewer Nicaraguans compared with Salvadoreans or Guatemalans were entering the United States without the required documentation through the San Diego sector. In fiscal year 1984, only 54 Nicaraguan nationals were deported from the United States (SYB 1984: 211). More recent reports indicate that large numbers of discontented youth are leaving Nicaragua to avoid the military draft:

After the elections [in late 1984], the number of people illegally leaving the country sharply increased. In early 1985, the Costa Rican minister of public security announced that in three days, three thousand Nicaraguan youth had entered his country. "Before the refugees were *campesinos*—but now we're getting young people from the city." Many of them were escaping the draft, which was imposed on young people over fifteen in 1983 and became an acute issue throughout the country in 1984. [Leiken 1986: 43]

Three of my male informants explicitly admitted having left Nicaragua to avoid a military draft that, they said, would mean eventually facing the contra war along the Honduran border.

In summary, there is ample evidence to document the political terror and severe economic scarcity currently prevailing in Central America. The personal experiences of all my informants had been in some measure directly affected by these conditions. Members of immigrant families most often cited as their reason for leaving *la situación* an increasing sense that the random political violence would sooner or later hit home. Some, chiefly Salvadorean and Guatemalan informants, had fled following the actual murder or disappearance of a relative, friend, or acquaintance (Vlach 1984). One family had escaped from El Salvador after the father, a factory guard, was assassinated. Another family left Guatemala after the killing of a cousin. Still others left El Salvador after colleagues began to disappear, only to have their mutilated corpses reappear. Some families, particularly Salvadorean and Nicaraguan, were directly escaping a random military draft that would force a youth to participate in what they deemed senseless slaughter. Eight of my 50 families reported a member escaping the draft. In addition, two Salvadoreans reported escaping aggressive guerrilla recruitment campaigns and terror. Two more families, both from El Salvador, reported escaping after a member of the family had been tortured by security officers. "Heidi," a Nicaraguan informant, cited the increasing communist agenda of the Sandinistas as her reason for leaving—particularly as it was reflected in their educational programs. The families from all three countries also cited economic motives for leaving *la situación*.

The Culture of Terror

Ernesto's story illuminates the human side of these cold statistics of pain. He left his native town in El Salvador during the bloodbath of 1981, and five years later he had completed his first semester at a leading U.S. university.

The situation in my country was the reason I left. My mother was very worried about my future, she was afraid about my safety. I came here all by myself, because as you know the situation in my country was bad. I did not like politics—any politics. There were many murdered without any reasons. . . . I was really afraid. Two of my cousins and two friends were killed, murdered in 1979, we couldn't believe it. And many acquaintances . . . just disappeared. People were killed by both sides, the death squads and the guerrillas. So one cannot be with one group or with the other; the best thing is to be quiet and not be involved in anything.

But then what happened to my friends made me afraid. I said "Any time something will happen to me. El Salvador is a place where it is a sin to be young." Life became impossible; I could no longer live like that. . . . I would go to school, and the students would be protesting about something, and the next day a few would be dead. . . . I was afraid I was going to be recruited into the army. There they teach you to be a criminal; they teach you to kill, kill, kill. They make you crazy. The death squads are sadists. They kill anyone. I thought of that when I came here; why should I go into gangs and get into fights if I escaped El Salvador to avoid all that?

Ernesto and also Ivan, both from rural El Salvador, were intelligent, energetic youths who became direct targets of the recruiting campaigns of both sides of the Salvadorean conflict. Ernesto remembers the terror of being caught in the live cross fire:

The *guerrilleros* they also looked for me; they wanted to take me along. I remember when they took my best friend, they beat him up, they mistreated him, they tied him up for hours. And they asked him about me, where I lived, what was I doing and all that. He would not tell them, so they tied him up and mistreated him more. When he finally told me all this, I was terrorized. I was nervous. The *guerrilleros* wanted me to be a leader in one of their groups. You see, they knew that I was a good student in school. They knew that, and they wanted me to be a leader. I always stayed away from politics.

I was also afraid of the death squads. They killed two of my cousins, they killed them without any reason! I don't know why they killed them, there is no reason at all. I was 14 years old and I saw all this.

Caught in the webs of a culture of terror (Taussig 1987: 3–135), both Ernesto and Ivan picked up and left the country at an early age for the journey to the United States. Once in the safety of the United States, their fears turned to the fate of relatives and friends left behind.

As the contra war against the Nicaraguan Sandinistas began to intensify in the early 1980's, and reports of random executions of innocent civilians became widespread (Dickey 1987; Neier 1986; Joseph and Wells 1985), Sandro's father, Don José, told him, "Well, we lived through one war [the war to overthrow Somoza]; I can't last through another one." So they left, to join Sandro's older sister who had been living in the United States for more than ten years. Sandro wanted to avoid entering a war foreign to him: "I won't go to the Honduran border to kill or be killed for a government I am personally against," he said. Although he was apolitical, he said that he did not like to see the increasing militarization of the country following the Sandinista takeover. "The military service there is like anywhere else in the world. The problem is that in Nicaragua there was never a draft. The country was not militarized. We know what the military can do. . . . Now the people don't like the military. When they wrote the new [draft] law, everyone was against it. We don't like to see the military everywhere."*

Alejandra, also from Managua, simply reported: "We left because of the [military] draft. You know that now they also draft women. Well, my family was against that; they would not have me go into a war." Many of her friends, she said, had also left Nicaragua, mostly to escape the draft. Another Nicaraguan informant reported that young women were also drafted to help in the coffee harvest.

Roberto, an 18-year-old Salvadorean youth, represents perhaps a more classic example of migration. His father had left El Salvador for the United States in late 1978; his grandmother and his aunt had been in the United States for over twenty years. Because his grandmother had become a U.S. citizen, she was able to request a permanent residence visa for her son, Roberto's father. Eventually the papers came through, and in 1978 Roberto's father left for the United States with the encouragement of his sister, who "would write telling us that if we worked hard here we could get ahead. That is why we came. He came first. Once the situation in El Salvador became very bad, he wanted us to follow him. He wanted us to study here." Roberto, his mother, and four siblings finally joined the father in the United States in 1981.

Pedro, a senior from El Salvador, had had bad luck. He was one of two informants who had been physically tortured by the security forces. He remembers that he was out playing soccer with his two cousins and a group of friends when the army picked them up. "It was a bad day; they were out looking for demonstrators," he later realized. They were taken to what he thought was a military installation; there they were tortured. Pedro and his friends were severely beaten, kicked in the stomach, and burned with cigarette butts. The soldiers kept asking him for the names and addresses of "other subversives." He tried to tell his captors that he was not involved, that he knew no one, that he and his pals were out just playing soccer. They were kept in detention for a few days without formal charges and were frequently terrorized. Pedro's parents eventually dis-

---

*For a recent overview of the Sandinista militarization of Nicaragua, see Leiken 1986.

covered where they were being held. Through their networks, and with the help of a human-rights organization, they were able to gain the boys' release. Before releasing Pedro, however, his captors told him, "This time you escape; next time we'll kill you." He summarized his tale of horror quite simply: "You know, the crime is being young." Whether being young is a crime or a sin, as Ernesto put it, the fact remains that youth are particularly at risk in the context of war (see Rosenblatt 1984).

Soon after this incident, Pedro's mother contacted his older brother, who had been living in the United States since the early 1970's. In 1981 Pedro's brother went back to El Salvador to get Pedro out. His cousins remain in El Salvador. They did not have the advantage of a brother in the United States who could take them away to a safer world. At the time of this research, Pedro was living with his older brother and his brother's wife and their two children in a tiny one-room studio in an inner city in the Southwest. In school he was having some paradoxical problems. His teachers liked him very much because he was polite and obedient, but he seemed to have problems with his peers. A few months after his arrival Pedro got into a fight with a classmate, apparently over a girlfriend, and allegedly assaulted the other fellow with a knife. He was kicked out of school. "You see, they *are* violent," Joaquin's bilingual counselor told me. No one in the school had referred Pedro to a counseling service to deal with the trauma of torture, separation from members of his nuclear family, and the stress of resettling in a new land. In fact, his psychological tests, like those of many new immigrants, capture a disturbing preoccupation with death and torture.*

The Legacy of Terror

Many new arrivals remained deeply affected by the morbid Central American scenario they had escaped. Ernesto, for example, became possessed by the horror that descended upon his land following the 1979 military coup and returned repeatedly to the workings of terror in our interviews:

* For a consideration of state-incited torture in El Salvador, see Brown 1985; Amnesty International 1984; for an anthropological treatment of torture and assassination in El Salvador, see Diskin 1985.

During the last six months there . . . I would have the same nightmare night after night. I dreamt that the death squads would come to my house to kill my family. . . . If they get you, the best thing that can happen is that they shoot you at once. But they torture you, they pull out your fingernails with pliers. They skinned the faces of people. They break all the bones in each hand. I saw that. I saw a man dead; they took his eyes out of the face and cut his ears off. They also burned his face with cigarettes and took out his fingernails. It was monstrous.

My own friends in the army would tell me what they did. The army and the death squads are the same thing. . . They look for people and kill them at night. I was afraid even though there was nothing I was guilty of; I was afraid.

I would be terrorized at night. Any little noise would scare me. I had this nightmare that the death squads came to our house. They would shoot their way through the door with machine guns. We were all taken to the back of the house, and they would sadistically kill each one in my family. First they killed my father, then my mother, then my little brother, and when it was my turn to die, I would wake up, shaking. Now I don't have this nightmare any more; here I am secure. Sometimes I do dream my family [father, mother, and younger brother remain in El Salvador] has problems. I worry about them. I dream that they came by to mistreat them, to rob them. I dream that. Before it was much worse, at night I could not sleep.

We were terrorized when the fighting came to our area. Once the guerrillas came to our neighborhood to steal food and money. And then the death squads would work at night. I was afraid. They never came to our house, but I was still afraid. They would look for guerrilleros. And the guerrilleros would take our money.

As a Kafkian character on trial by his own unconscious mind, Ernesto's fears followed him day and night and he became a captive of the culture of terror, although he was innocent. He felt terrorized and was castigated by an inner voice quoting the outer madness.

Collective fear, like other cultural systems, may be said to possess an underlying structure, its own grammar, as it were. The calculated unleashing of terror seems first to bring about a shared numbing hysteria in a population, to be followed by increasing defensive rationalizations about local events and, eventually, by the internalization of fear. Psychosocially, the culture of fear operates through the unconscious, so that its victims are afraid even though they have no guilt. Facing the unspeakable all around, the fragile ego contains the "unmaking of the world" (Scarry 1985) in torture and dirty wars by engaging in (1) hysterical denials ("we couldn't believe it") followed by ultimately unconvincing (2) rationalizations for survival ("the best thing [to survive] is to be quiet and not be involved in anything"; "I did not like politics—any politics"). Finally, when the imminent danger subsides, when one escapes these nightmarish dirty wars, the fear returns in the form of a new consciousness of events and images previously denied and repressed. The result is an almost compulsive need to talk about what was once forbidden. This last phase is the internalization of terror.*

A preoccupation with death, torture, and assassination was a major legacy of the Central American culture of terror for some new arrivals. In the Thematic Apperception Test (TAT) stories I collected, there is indeed a statistical overrepresentation of these concerns, as compared with other samples. A number of researchers have used the TAT in the course of their ethnographic work.† My interest in the TAT is *not* as a clinical, psychodiagnostic tool, nor is it in individual idiosyncrasies, but rather in the shared, patterned thematic perceptual clusters found in a given population.

The TAT consists of a series of 30 pictures that are presented sequentially to the informant.‡ The informant is simply asked to make up a story, out of the imagination, to give a narrative with a past, a present, and a future based on what he/she sees in the pictures. The TAT rests on the logic that informants, presented with vague stimuli, will reveal their interpersonal attitudes and ongoing concerns. The narratives they create will reflect their own wishes, fears, dreams, and worries. The test, when given to specific populations, can be used to postulate normative patterns of preoccupation for the group as a whole. Some scholars have argued that it may serve as a powerful tool complementing participant observation and ethnographic interviews to systematically elicit certain key, shared concerns, or the interpersonal "atmospheric condition" of a given cultural group that may not

* For an account of the Argentine Culture of Terror during the so-called dirty war in the 1970's, see Timerman 1981; Suarez-Orozco 1987d.
† See, e.g., Rabkin 1987; Wagatsuma and De Vos 1984; De Vos 1983a, 1973; Scheper-Hughes 1979; Lindzey 1961; Banfield 1958; Henry 1956.
‡ See pp. 106 and 119 for reproductions of TAT Cards 1 and 2.

be immediately visible or easily approached through other means of research (Scheper-Hughes 1979; De Vos 1973; Lindzey 1961). The TAT, then, serves as a medium to allow informants to explore certain emotional issues in a manner that is less threatening than, for example, direct questioning. A variety of basic concerns such as shared attitudes toward achievement among Koreans and Japanese (see De Vos 1983*a*; 1973), changing attitudes among kibbutzniks on the nature of their venture (see Rabkin 1987), the fatalism of southern Italians (see Banfield 1958), and rural Irish attitudes toward sexuality (Scheper-Hughes 1979) have been elegantly documented with the TAT.

Other scholars, however, within both the academic psychology and the anthropology disciplines, have argued that the TAT, like other projective techniques, is subject to a number of criticisms, particularly when it is utilized in ethnographic fieldwork. Some of the critiques, according to Lindzey, are unwarranted or overgeneralized, and some are on target (1961: 178, 182, 189). A major unwarranted assault on the projective technique in general is that it comes between the observer and his basic data—human behavior (Lindzey 1961: 179). This is clearly irrelevant to my findings because the TAT was administered only after months of field work, and after I had recorded large amounts of basic data derived from participant observation and formal interviews. I would note that projective tests, when used properly and in addition to other standard anthropological tools, make more work for the anthropologist, who must spend long hours to collect a sample of stories and then to transcribe, order, and analyze them.* There is no reason why responses to a projective test should not be considered valid "human behavior" for anthropological analysis.

Another criticism is that the "use of *projective techniques* tend to impose upon the anthropologist the *language of pathology*" (Lindzey 1961: 183). The fear in this context is that the "psychiatric ward" terminology derivative of the clinical use of these tests would somehow contaminate the final ethnographic record. This is not a real concern here, given the purpose for which

---

* All TAT stories were collected in Spanish, the language in which my informants felt most comfortable. All stories were recorded on audio tape and were translated by a Mexican professional translator who was unfamiliar with the overall nature of the research.

the data are analyzed. Terms such as "achievement motivation," "concern over nurturance," "affiliation," or "concern over torture" are hardly psychopathological terms. There is also criticism of the degree of randomness of a sample derived from a given population. My sample is not based on rigorous random sampling, since there were strictures in establishing contact and gaining access to informants. Any criticism of sampling can be applied to anthropological observation as a whole. Traditionally anthropologists have hardly gone about selecting their key informants at random. Indeed, some major anthropological works are renowned for their heavy reliance on the expertise of relatively few informants (for a recent example, see Shostak 1983). In this case, some anthropologists, themselves traditionally predisposed against psychological approaches and concepts in anthropology, may be using a double standard. For example, collectors of folklore and other cultural data make little attempt to demonstrate statistically how such information or interests are distributed throughout a given population. Lastly, "even among projective-technique experts, there is *no agreement on how these techniques should be analyzed and interpreted*" (Lindzey 1961: 185). There is indeed no universal agreement over how to analyze projective data, but some scholars (De Vos 1973, 1981; Scheper-Hughes 1979) advocate setting explicit criteria for coding narrative materials within a culturally specific framework that can be then checked by others.

The TAT data presented here were systematically analyzed following a "system of codification for interpersonal concerns in thematic or narrative materials" devised by De Vos (1981). Subsequent to my first scoring of the data, De Vos "blindly" scored responses to the cards analyzed below. This system of codification is concerned with establishing reliability of scoring on the basis of the manifest content of a story. Latent psychodynamic processes are not a major concern. Rather than searching for hidden deep structures or the Basic Personality Structure in a sample, the system serves to identify the main thematic issues in narratives as they unfold in the syntagmatic or sequential order given by the informants. In the broadest terms, this system heuristically divides human behavior into "instrumentally" oriented behavior (means to an end) and expressive behavior (end in and of itself). Within the system are several categories of concern that order the data around universal themes in interpersonal behavior that are found in every culture. Examples of instrumental concerns are achievement-alienation, competence-incompetence, responsibility-irresponsibility, control-subordination, and co-operation-competition. Expressive concerns relate to nurturance-deprivation, harmony-discord, affiliation-isolation, pleasure-suffering, and appreciation-degradation (De Vos 1981). Clusters of such thematic concerns in the stories are then treated numerically, and their occurrence can be compared to that in other cultural groups. It is essential that any projective test be used only in the context of other data, careful interviewing, and ethnographic observation. The anthropologist must be intimate enough with the culture and the language to interpret the findings emerging from the projective materials. Therefore, the TAT should not be used before the researcher has established adequate communication with the informant.

The theme of how torture, assassination, and death emerged as disturbing concerns in the projective life of my informants was captured most forcefully in Card 8BM of the TAT, which I administered to 42 informants. In the foreground of the picture, there is an adolescent boy. The barrel of a rifle is visible at one side, and in the background is the dim scene of a surgical operation, like a reverie-image (Murray 1943: 19). This card usually elicits stories of an operation, an accident, or the achievement reveries of a youth contemplating a medical career. In the Central American sample of 42 informants, however, themes of torture, with resultant fear, rare or completely absent in other samples, appeared in nineteen of the stories.

"A torture, he is looking at how a young man is suffering. . . . They are cutting off the man's arm."

"People torturing the guy on the table. . . . I see weapons."

"He remembers the torture he saw. The atrocities men can commit."

"He remembers when he saw them hurt a relative. He tries to forget. He is afraid he will go mad."

"He remembers when his brother was assassinated."

TABLE 3.1

Summary of Central American Immigrants' Responses to TAT Card 8BM,
by Sex and Age

(*N* = 42)

Theme	Male/Female by Age Group				Percent of Total Responses
	M 14–16 (*n* = 10)	F 14–16 (*n* = 6)	M 17–19 (*n* = 17)	F 17–19 (*n* = 9)	
Torture and assas-sination	5	3	7	4	45.2%
Goal of becoming a doctor	2	1	2	1	14.3
Hero as protagonist	0	1	1	1	7.2
Hero in operation	1	0	4	2	16.7
Other	0	0	1	0	2.3
Rejected card	2	1	2	1	14.3

NOTE: Korean immigrants responded as follows to this card: torture and assassination 0 percent; goal of becoming a doctor 28 percent; hero as protagonist 26 percent; hero in operation 46 percent (De Vos 1983*a*).

"He was afraid, he saw someone's death. His parents sent him to a psychologist for help."

In six of the remaining stories, the boy wishes to be a surgeon; he is a protagonist in a movie (3); he is undergoing an operation (4), or is a witness to an operation (3). In one story the adolescent boy is dreaming about a gang fight. Finally, six informants rejected the card, a most unusual occurrence in sampling with the TAT (Table 3.1). The fact that so large a percentage of my informants articulated stories of this nature confirms the impression that escaping from political terror has left a profound legacy of internal pain in the psyche of many of the recent arrivals.* As I became increasingly aware of the magnitude of this occurrence, I administered Card 8BM to ten recent immigrants from Mexico for purposes of comparison. They too had entered the country within the past five years, were enrolled in the same schools as the Central Americans, and were in the same age-range and general socioeconomic status. Yet not one of the Mexican stories had a theme of torture or assassination. In most of their stories

* For a consideration of posttraumatic stress disorder among new arrivals from war-torn Central America, see Arroyo and Eth 1985.

the boy was dreaming that he would become a doctor (4), or fighting regular criminals (1), or witnessing an operation on a relative (1); or he was a hospital worker in a war situation (1), or he was being operated on because he was very ill (2). Only one of the ten Mexican immigrants rejected the card.

Two additional factors underline the profound significance of this finding among recent Central American immigrants. First, of Korean immigrants sampled (see Table 3.1, note), not one informant produced a narrative specifically involving torture. And in only 13 of their stories is there a theme of aggression, such as the avenging of the death of a father or a friend. The majority of the stories are in fact about achievement. Second, among the Central Americans in my sample the theme of torture, massacres, and assassinations surfaced again spontaneously in responses to other TAT cards. For example, Card 9BM, where four men in overalls are lying on the grass "taking it easy" (Murray 1943: 19), evoked themes of torture and massacre in three of the 40 stories. Such stories are also absent in other samples, where the imagery elicited is commonly one of relaxation: "This looks like Nicaragua when they killed the peasants." "They kidnapped a boy; they are hurting him. He is trying to escape." "Bodies . . . They are in a civil war. They are all dead. Assassinated." From Card 7BM, which usually elicits themes of mentorship or father-son relations—a gray-haired man is looking at a younger man sullenly staring into space—three stories likewise refer to violence: "Two men plot to assassinate somebody. They assassinate him. They were picked up by the police and tortured." "They are talking about killing somebody. They kill him." "He is pressuring the young man to hurt some one. He does it. He is captured."

These stories are isomorphic narratives of the pain that often surfaced during random conversations and systematic interviews with the recent arrivals. Yet, throughout an entire year of fieldwork I did not once hear a teacher or a counselor deal with this preoccupation as a potential influence on any student's social adaptation. In Pedro's case—he was himself a victim of torture—psychological services to deal with the lasting effects of his experience were never urged on him, so far as I know. Eventually he exploded and was kicked out of school for assaulting another student with a knife.

Another informant, Jorge, who was also greatly troubled, received no counseling. He was a 15-year-old from El Salvador
under the supervision of his elderly grandmother, who worked
as a live-in maid. When Jorge's father was killed in El Salvador,
his mother, who could no longer take care of him, had sent him
to live with his paternal grandmother in the United States. Because of her job, he went virtually unsupervised for days. A
teacher pointed him out at an early stage of the study as a "typical loser." He was a perennial class-cutter. He shared a minuscule apartment in the inner city with another young man from El
Salvador, a few years older than himself. Eventually, I found out
that he would often just stay home alone, day after day. When I
asked him why he cut classes so often, he said he was bored in
school and had no energy to learn English. He appeared to be in
the midst of a depression, but to the school experts he was a
typical Latino loser.

In summary, then, we have placed certain key interpersonal
concerns and reflections of a number of informants against the
larger context of life in war-torn Central America. Escaping a
world of political terror and limited economic opportunities has
profound, patterned effects upon subsequent functioning in the
United States. The psychological energy invested in dealing
with this legacy is not conducive to optimal school functioning,
yet I observed no efforts on the part of the schools to ameliorate
the pain of the victims. Upon entering their new land, students
have had to contend with their own remembrances as well as
with the ongoing conditions still affecting those left behind.
Considering this legacy and the fact that their entry into the U.S.
urban society was through the atmosphere of the inner city, it is
most remarkable that any of the recent arrivals stayed in school
and tried to learn the new language at all. At the conscious level,
their psychological journey from the land of scarcity and terror
to the inner city gives rise to a clear awareness of the relative
advantages of life in the host society over life at home, particularly among the older, more mature informants in my sample.
Ivan reflected on the meaning of his longitudinal and cross-
cultural experience:

Now I often think back about my country. I think about what would
have happened to me had I stayed there. Now I think that the guerrillas

would have taken me away. . . . In my country the military have the power. Militarism rules. This is what I now see. If you say any little thing against the government, later you show up dead. Now I see the difference. Here you have the right to say anything that pleases you. . . and nothing will happen to you. Also you can get ahead, you can better yourself here. . . .

Here you don't find the kind of life you find in El Salvador. In this country there is freedom. This is what I love about this country. In this country anyone can become anything they like. . . .

I never thought I would . . . have the opportunity to learn English. And look at me now: I speak English and I have an American high school diploma. So, I see that I was given these opportunities and that I did achieve something.

A few months after this chat, Ivan began studying at a local college. When I inquired what this meant to him, he seemed a little puzzled, but then replied that this would give him the opportunity eventually to help his family in El Salvador. He was referring to his arthritic mother who sells goods in the local market, his father who works for the post office, and his three younger brothers, still likely targets for guerrilla and/or army recruitment. "They made it possible for me to be here," he said softly, as if it should have been obvious to me.

FOUR

Parental Sacrifice

AMONG THE IMMIGRANT youngsters perhaps the major concern emerging in the context of leaving *la situación* at home was related to the efforts and sacrifices made by parents and other folk in order to send them to the safety of the United States. According to many informants, parents suffered great hardships, often investing precious and limited resources to finance the journey north. Among those informants with parents or siblings still in Central America, the issue of familial sacrifice also emerged as significant: not only had they made supreme efforts, but they also continued to live in fear and deprivation. Amadeo, for example, was well aware of the campaign his parents had to mount to send him out of Nicaragua, to avoid the military draft. "They had to move mountains," he said, referring to the briberies and other costs involved in leaving his country. And Ivan, whose home had been in El Salvador, was concerned about the welfare of his family:

I would not be so worried about them if they were here with me. I get headaches thinking about their life in El Salvador. I worry about them. Last time I talked to my father [on the telephone], he told me the guerrilleros came to our house and took all their money, grain, and other stuff. He had to give them money or they would kill him right there. . . . The guerrilleros say, "You must help the revolution," and they take your money. And if you refuse they kill you right there on the spot. . . .

My parents go on working and what for? From sunrise to sunset . . . working their little land. That's their life there. I worry. I also worry about my brothers. I am afraid they would take them away to the war. That is why I want to bring them here with me as soon as I can.

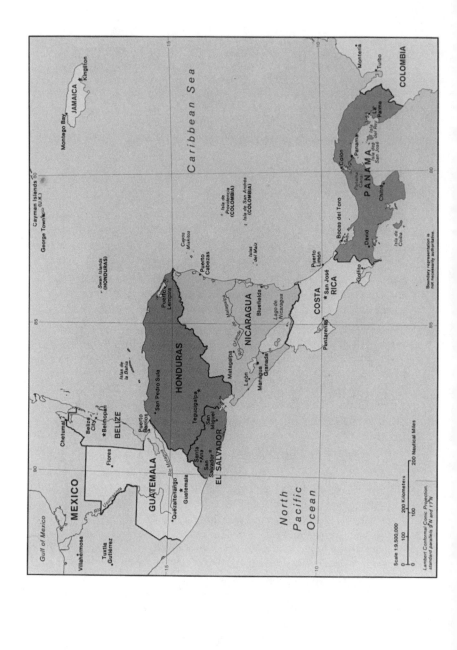

Vlach, in her study of immigrant families recently arrived to the United States from Guatemala, reports a similar pattern of continued concern over those left behind:

Ana Lucia [informant] is still quite worried about conditions at home for her family [in Guatemala]. She feels guilty for being here while many of her relatives have reported difficulties they have had. A cousin of hers was shot and injured in a terrorist attack; his house was also burned to the ground. Her youngest sister with whom she is the closest attempted to come to the U.S. and was caught by the authorities and deported back to Guatemala. . . . Finally, Ana Lucia has received letters recently from family members which have stated that her mother is ill with gastritis and is quite weak. [1984: 155]

Guilt, unlike Ana Lucia's younger sister, travels across borders rather easily.

Such perceptions of parental sacrifice became an intricate factor in a patterned motivational system. The strong desire in many immigrants to work and study, to remain in an educational system unlike their own, to learn English, to enter college or professional training, or to secure a good-paying job was firmly rooted in a familial matrix of reciprocity and mutual nurturance. In the view of many informants, their parents had given up a great deal to establish them in this country. It was now up to them to take full advantage of the emerging opportunities in the new land, to "become somebody" (*llegar a ser alguien*), as they would put it. This wish to maximize emerging opportunities was far removed from an individualistic wish for independence or self-advancement. Rather, the aim of many youths was to place themselves in an advantageous situation in order to care properly for their parents and other less fortunate family members back home.

The parents for their part made it clear that it was now the student's turn to reciprocate by making good on the opportunity to study and be trained in the United States, an opportunity many of the parents had never enjoyed. Many of the parents whom I came to know made no effort to hide the fact that they had endured great hardships so the children could have a better tomorrow. As the research progressed, it became evident that the motivation and the effort to succeed were intertwined with an express wish to pay parents back for their sacrifices. This theme surfaced quite strongly in Card 2 of the Thematic Apperception Test.

During my work as Joaquin's parent/community liaison, I came into daily contact with many parents, guardians, relatives, and friends of students, especially recent arrivals from Central America. I met with them to find out problem areas; to help mediate between monolingual Spanish-speaking parents and monolingual English-speaking teachers; to counsel parents on educational issues; to serve as a resource linking parents with community agencies that offered all kinds of educational services, from adult education classes to after-school ESL tutoring for their children. In short, I was a bilingual pedagogical troubleshooter. It was in this capacity that I first learned from the parents and others of the efforts that went into escaping terror and surviving in a foreign land.

Ms. Smith, an ESL teacher, asked me to get in touch with the parents of Claudia Cariño, a 14-year-old from Nicaragua. After a relatively good performance during the prior semester, Claudia was now "goofing off." She had been cutting class quite systematically, and when she did come to class, she was often late. The teacher wanted me to find out what the problem was. Her own hunch was that Claudia was probably working at night, like many of the other immigrant students, and that she was therefore probably too tired early in the morning to make it to class. As it turned out, the teacher was mistaken.

During those months of work at Joaquin High I learned that, contrary to the notion of many teachers in the inner-city classroom, the parents and guardians of these Hispanic youths were greatly interested in the education of their children. They were ready to help in any way they could, but felt it was presumptuous of them to take too much initiative when it came to school matters. After all, they carried with them from Central America a deep respect for the teaching profession, and their working assumption was that teachers knew best. They would stand by and be ready to collaborate should the teacher request their involvement, but volunteering was beyond their cultural repertoire. The problem was that the teachers, used to parental volunteerism, would expect the same initiative from immigrant parents, which was not forthcoming. This cultural miscommunication was translated by many teachers as, "You see, they don't care about schooling."

Parents did care a great deal and, when contacted, they were very willing to act. I cannot recall a single instance, for example, when a parent, an aunt, or an older brother missed an appointment with me to go over some educational issue. In fact, I had arranged that Claudia's mother come to see me at 8 A.M. one Tuesday in February. When I arrived at the school at about 7:50 A.M. I discovered that she had been waiting for me outside the main gate since 6:30 A.M. Because she did not trust public transportation, her husband, who had to be at work at 7:00 A.M., had dropped her off on his way.

Mrs. Cariño was in her mid-fifties, and seemed anxious to tell me her story. They had come to the United States a bit over a year before, from Nicaragua, where life for poor people was hard, she said. She had been a nurse's aide, and her husband an electrician. There had been all sorts of shortages, including food, medicines, and clothing. The new draft law disturbed them a great deal, especially since she, as a nurse's aide, had seen at first hand the consequences of the ongoing war; and she had four children who would eventually be drafted. The escalating Contra war against the Sandinistas made it likely that her children, when drafted, would see combat on the Nicaraguan-Honduran border. Correspondence and telephone communication with her older sister, who had been established in the United States for years, convinced Mrs. Cariño and her husband that it was time to leave Nicaragua. The exodus had been hard. He had left a year before the rest of the family and stayed at first with her sister. Upon finding steady work and a small apartment, he began saving money to bring his wife and four children into the United States. In the meantime, Mrs. Cariño herself worked extra hours at the hospital to save money for the journey. Leaving her country was very hard for her, she said. She spoke no English and could not continue in her profession. Her husband also had to take a cut in status: whereas he had been an electrical foreman in a large Nicaraguan industrial plant, he was now an electrician in a small family-run appliance repair shop owned by Americans of Hispanic descent. Regardless, he was thankful that he could remain in his profession. She, on the other hand, had to become a maid.

As we began going over the specifics of Claudia's current problems, Mrs. Cariño told me she and her husband usually left for work at about 6:00 A.M. The other three children left for school at 8:00 A.M. Because Claudia had no class during the first period, she remained at home, all alone, until about 9:00 A.M. Obviously, her mother said, Claudia had just been staying home the entire day, probably watching television. Mrs. Cariño indicated that she had not been happy with this arrangement. She wished she could be at home to make certain that everyone left for school at the right time. As a compromise she would telephone her house from work at about 9:30 A.M. each day, to see if everyone had gone to school. She added, as if apologizing, that since no one would answer the telephone, she had been assuming that all the children, including Claudia, were safely in school. Claudia was simply not answering the telephone.

Mrs. Cariño was greatly disturbed about Claudia's behavior. "How can she do this?" she asked. She insisted that we talk directly to Claudia's teachers and ask for their advice. The ESL teacher could not see her at that moment, but Mr. Bozza, the bilingual mathematics teacher, was willing to meet with her on the spot. He too was concerned about Claudia's performance because he knew she was "bright and motivated . . . even enthusiastic about her work." The problem, as far as he was concerned, was that she just cut classes too often, seventeen times during the course of the current semester. Mrs. Cariño then asked me to call Claudia to be present during the rest of our meeting, and Mr. Bozza went back to his classroom. Claudia came into the office, sheepishly staring at the carpet. Her mother simply began reading aloud from Claudia's attendance record sheet, which I had given to her earlier. "Why don't you come to class?" she asked. Claudia, frozen in her seat, would not lift her eyes to face her mother or me. Finally, Mrs. Cariño asked, "Why do you do this to me?" She choked and began crying. Turning to me, as if to amplify her message to Claudia by bouncing it through my desk, Mrs. Cariño said, still crying,

They know how I sacrifice, cleaning houses everyday so that they can have a future here. . . . But I do it for them. And the only thing I ask of them is that they study, the only thing. I leave home at 6 A.M. and get back after dark so that they can have all they need. . . . They know all what we have been through to get here, and now instead of going forward she goes backward. . . . In Nicaragua they would have drafted them all into the army. That's why we are here—for them. . . . it is too late for me; at my age there is no future in this country. . . . But they— now *they* have a future. They know I have no future here, at my age with no English. But *they* have everything in front of them. . . . All they have to do is take advantage of it. I get them everything they need to study. I just bought them a computer so they can get ahead. I don't ask them to work, just to study, all they have to do is study.

Soon Claudia, who had remained paralyzed during her mother's speech, began weeping too.

I have presented in some detail this seemingly melodramatic sequence of a mother's attempt at control by arousing a sense of guilt because it is paradigmatic of a basic theme found in the lives of many recent immigrants from Central America. Mrs. Cariño has to run a household in a foreign country, operating in a language she understands only slightly, and unable to work in her profession. Life in the inner city, plagued with violence and other hazards, without the extended network of family and community was hard enough. Mrs. Cariño, like other parents, had become increasingly aware that life for them in the new land would most likely continue to be an endurance of recurring hardships—far removed from what informants fancied it would be like when they began preparing the journey to "El Norte."

She made this point forcefully. Upon her arrival, she had been full of energy and enthusiastic about learning English and soon enrolled in adult ESL classes at night. She would leave her house at 6 A.M. to work, clean houses until about 7 P.M., go home and make dinner with the help of her daughters, feed the family and rush out to night school to study English from 8:30 until 9:30. This routine was brutal. Soon, and much to her sorrow, she began facing the fact that she could not continue at this pace. Deciding to drop her ESL class was very hard for Mrs. Cariño. In a sense, it came to signify the fact that she could no longer justify all the immediate hardships with the dream that one day she would escape the cycle of hard work. Giving up her classes meant giving up the possibility of ever entering her profession in the United States; it condemned her to remaining a maid for the rest of her life in the host society. Still, she had her children. Sacrifice could be endured more directly in relation to the future opportunities *they* could seize in the host society. She became more conscious of the fact that the resettling effort was now more exclusively related to the children and their future.

Claudia had been "goofing off." She was depressed, increasingly discontented with school, and feeling a strong sense of inadequacy. At the beginning of her first semester in the United States, the owner of one of the houses cleaned by Mrs. Cariño had told Claudia that if she was able to earn an A during her first semester of American schooling, she would give her a $10 prize. By the end of the first semester Claudia had earned mostly B's and a few C's, but not a single A. When the time came to show the lady her grade card, Claudia felt a sense of shame and inadequacy over the fact that she failed to meet what was expected of her. Claudia concluded, "Me desanime" (I lost inspiration).

After the encounter in my office Claudia's attendance improved remarkably. Mrs. Cariño, Claudia's teachers, and I kept her under close watch during the rest of the year. The teachers eventually reported a significant improvement in her performance. Mrs. Cariño and I kept in weekly contact over her progress. Clearly, Claudia needed some reminding of the fact that her schoolwork was not merely a personal issue over a lost prize but rather a family affair, intimately related to the very meaning of the family's resettlement in the new land. It was part of a larger pattern of mutual interdependence and nurturance that became all the more evident when the parents picked up and left Nicaragua to offer the children a better tomorrow. Now it was Claudia's turn to deliver by studying and making progress in school.

Unlike Claudia, older informants spontaneously demonstrated a remarkable sense of responsibility to their parents that derived from their perceptions of parental sacrifice. A sense of guilt is specifically related to a wish to repay parents for previous, as well as ongoing, sacrifice. For specific reasons study and school performance were viewed as the ideal avenue to repay parents.

José, Estela, and Pedro stayed with their maternal grandmother in their rural Guatemalan village when their mother left for the United States in search of a better tomorrow. The children had not seen their father for years. They knew that he was a taxi driver, a heavy drinker, and a wife-beater. They thought he now lived in Guatemala City. Once in the United States their mother worked as a maid for a number of wealthy families until she landed "an easier job," also as a maid, in a downtown hotel. Eventually, she was able to save enough money to bring all her children into the United States. Her schedule was made all the more difficult by the fact that they lived in a small apartment in the inner city, far away from the hotel. In winter, she would leave for work while it was still dark. The mother insisted that the children not work, but devote themselves to study full time.

Estela was very busy at home, helping run the daily operations in the household; she would get up early every morning, before anyone else, and would make some breakfast for all. Upon return from school, she would clean up the apartment and prepare dinner; only then would she concentrate on her homework. When the mother came home, dinner would be ready and the apartment would be in order. José, the oldest, 17 years old, remained bothered that his mother had worked so hard for so long. Although he had an impeccable GPA and was a brilliant student, he was undecided whether to go to the university or whether to go to work full time:

My mother . . . has been here ten years. . . . Without even a high school diploma. She went only to the second grade of high school in Guatemala. Then she had to work. When she came here it was so hard for her. She was all alone with no family here. She spoke no English. I now want to help her, so she does not continue to work any more. . . . That is the only thing I have to do. This is why I am undecided about going to the University . . . or going to work. She wants me to do what I desire but. . . . Well, for me it would not be correct not to work because of the way she has helped us.

Even though his mother gives him the freedom to do what he desires, he views that exclusive attention to his needs as unacceptable. She had sacrificed until she was able to get her children out of misery in Guatemala. She then had continued to work hard so that her children could gain an education in the United States and become somebody. Her sacrifices place a specific psychological burden on the children. Her dream is that they be able to escape the cycle of ignorance and hardship that she herself had endured since childhood. Schooling in the United States emerges as the key avenue out of this cycle; it is the medium to become somebody, which is the immigrant's foremost plan and handy reason for rationalizing ongoing hardships.

In José's case a typical immigrant contradiction emerges. The perception of parental sacrifice fuels a wish to study and to do well in school, to take full advantage of the precious opportunities in the host country. At the same time, that perception made him, like other informants in similar situations, anxious to begin working at once to earn money, to ease the burden on his mother's shoulders. A few months later José and Pedro found a partial solution to this contradiction in a part-time job delivering newspapers every day from 6 A.M. until 8 A.M. They told their mother that delivering the papers before school would not interfere with their school work. All three children remained on the school's honor roll that entire year. The boys gave their earnings to their mother.

Beyond the immediate resettlement-related sacrifices endured by members of their families, numerous informants reported that their parents had had very difficult lives. As I became increasingly aware of the recurrence of this theme, I began to explore its roots and the possible implications for the immigrant's own current adaptation. Whenever I would ask informants to explain why their parents had had such difficult lives, they would invariably refer back to *la situación* in the country of origin. When I probed for elaboration beyond that, the informants would eventually mention their parents' lack of education. Once we isolated this theme, the narratives became repetitive: "Life in El Salvador was very hard when they were growing up; there were no schools in the countryside." "They could not study; they had to work to help their parents." "She was the oldest of eleven children; she had to work to help feed them." "He never went to school; he worked the land with his father since he was a child." "He could not go on studying; he had to work to help his parents." "Her father died when she was a child; she had to work to help her mother." Economic pressures had pushed parents out of school early in their lives (see Table 4.1), in most instances to work and help out their family.

TABLE 4.1

Highest Level of Education Completed by Parents

(N = 100)

Years of Schooling	El Salvador	Nicaragua	Guatemala	Percent
Mother (*n* = 50)				
4 years of college				
or more	0	2	1	6%
Some college	2	0	0	4
High school only	1	0	0	2
Some high school	5	3	2	20
Elementary school only	3	1	3	14
Some elementary school	15	1	1	34
No schooling	4	0	1	10
No data	3	1	1	10
TOTAL	33	8	9	100%
Father (*n* = 50)				
4 years of college				
or more	1	2	1	8%
Some college	5	1	1	14
High school only	2	2	2	12
Some high school	5	1	4	20
Elementary school only	2	2	1	10
Some elementary school	10	0	0	20
No schooling	3	0	0	6
No data	5	0	0	10
TOTAL	33	8	9	100%

A large percentage of the recent arrivals reported that their parents had been unable to complete school.* Among the mothers in this sample, 78 percent had not completed a high-school education, and of the Salvadorean mothers in the sample, over half (57.5 percent) had not completed an elementary education in the country of origin. None of the Salvadorean mothers in my sample graduated from college; two of them enrolled briefly in college, one in psychology and the other one in Letters, but did not graduate. Among the Nicaraguan mothers, 62.5 percent had less than a complete high school education. Two of the Nicaraguan mothers had graduated from college, one in education, the other in accounting. Among the Guatemalan mothers, 77.8 per-

* These figures reflect the fact that in general my sampling avoided upper-class families.

cent had less than a complete high school education. Only one Guatemalan mother graduated from college, also in accounting. In short, this sample confirms a common observation from my youthful informants that the parents for a variety of reasons had been unable to study as much or for as long as they had desired.

The majority of the fathers in my sample, over 55 percent, had been unable to earn a high school diploma. Of the Salvadorean fathers, 39.4 percent had not completed an elementary education in the country of origin. At the same time, 18.2 percent of all Salvadorean fathers did study beyond high school. Among the Nicaraguan fathers, the group in this sample with the most schooling, 37.5 percent went beyond high school. Coincidentally, 37.5 percent of the Nicaraguan fathers had less than a high-school diploma. Although my Nicaraguan sample is small (eight families), it seems to reflect the observation that recent arrivals from this country tend to be from the more educated segment of the society. Among the Guatemalan fathers, 55.5 percent had less than a complete high-school education. At the same time, 22.2 percent of the Guatemalan fathers had studied beyond the high-school level in their country of origin.

Many parents directly and spontaneously stated that they had moved so that their children could have a better tomorrow through schooling in the host society. Angel, now attending a major U.S. university, exemplifies this theme. He had come to the United States with his mother and older sister during a crescendo of killing in his native El Salvador in the early 1980's. He graduated from high school with a cumulative GPA of 3.74. In fact, all during his American schooling he had been on the honor roll. Rafaela, Angel's mother, worked as a maid and did not allow him to work during the academic year. She noted that they came to the United States "so that he can study in peace and make a better tomorrow here." Rafaela made it clear that she wanted him to dedicate himself totally to study. War and a wrecked economy in El Salvador had pushed away any fantasies that her children could escape repeating her modest existence of hard work and little reward. And she herself was keenly aware of what life without an education was like: she had had to leave school during the elementary school years to begin a long history in service. Angel himself was conscious of why she was now so anxious that he study: "She does not want me to lead a life such as the one they had to live when they were young. They had to work hard, sacrifice themselves."

Perceptions of parental sacrifice surfaced as a basic theme in my informants' responses to Card 2 of the TAT (see Table 7.1). In more than 50 percent of these narratives, my informants pictured the parental *dramatis personae* as living in poverty and enduring severe hardships. Murray's manual for the TAT describes Card 2 as "a country scene: in the foreground is a young woman with books in her hand, in the background a man is working in the fields and an older woman is looking on" (1943: 19). Scarcity in the form of poverty, not found in the Anglo-American, Japanese, or Korean immigrant samples (see De Vos 1973; 1983*a*), is the key theme that the scene elicited from my informants. Their stories lead us to the conclusion that this recurring theme is a major preoccupation at the conscious level: "This is about the great efforts people make to survive in a poor environment." "She sees misery all around her. Her sister is pregnant, and her husband is working hard. . . . Her father helped her go to a city to study." "A poor village. He must work very hard and earns very little money to send his children to study, to prepare themselves." "Her parents were poor peasants. They . . . endured hard work all their lives. They did all they could to help her study." "The man is struggling. They struggle so hard in life. They live in poverty."

In summary, then, it is evident that perceptions of parental sacrifice are intertwined with achievement motivation. A pattern of mutuality and interdependence emerges that exhibits a basic continuity: as their parents had helped their own folks, so now did many informants feel it was their turn to help their parents to achieve a better future.

The journey north brought a new array of hardships and difficulties. Upon arrival in the affluent society, the immigrant parents entered the lowest levels of the occupational structure. They became maids, janitors, babysitters, dishwashers, cook's helpers, bellboys, gardeners, laundromat operators, waitresses, cashiers, and factory workers. Those few who were educated in their countries suffered a loss of status as they entered the U.S. labor market. An engineer became a high school math tutor; an accountant became a bank teller; a college professor became a Spanish tutor in the local high school.

As they resettled in the inner city, parents began to fully appreciate the nature of the hardships they would continue to endure. They found themselves operating in a foreign culture, in a language they barely understood, often not possessing the required documentation for permanent residence. The jobs they were able to secure were in the lower levels of the opportunity structure. These were hard, poorly paying jobs. Increasingly aware of the hard reality of the inner city, many of these parents psychologically turned to their children as their hope for a better future. The question then arises: How would the youngsters attain that better future? To maximize opportunity through schooling would be the key.

FIVE

Here and There:
The Immigrant's Dual Frame
of Reference

NOW WE MOVE to explore how the immigrants came to think
and feel about themselves and their new setting, and how migration afforded many of them a dual perspective on the nature
of their unfolding lives. As they made sense of their current reality, they often paused to make reflective statements comparing a
given issue in the two social contexts: their past home and the
new host society. Specifically, education emerged as the key to
their future plans.

Despite experiencing new hardships in the inner city, most of
my informants remained convinced that they had far more and
better opportunities to become somebody in the United States
than in Central America. Although life in the affluent society
never quite turned out to be what they had expected, the process of adaptation to a new sociocultural atmosphere gave birth
to an immigrant ethic among the youth in which perceptions
of opportunity seemed to overshadow hardship. The earliest
change in worldview occurs as the immigrants enter the inner
city. At this point, many of the fantasies carried in their baggage
from home are found to have no substance. As the informants
became more conversant with inner-city culture and social structure, they developed a more somber, but yet more favorable view
of future opportunities.

Reality and Anticipation in the Inner City

Before migration, as the situation in Central America became increasingly intolerable for many informants and their families, their feelings and expectations of life in the United States became increasingly idealized. It seems that the harder their daily life in Central America became, the glossier their picture of life in the United States. The north eventually became a not-so-distant mirror of serenity and affluence.

A number of informants reported entering the United States with exaggerated, indeed almost fantastic, views of life in the affluent society. Herman, who had left El Salvador when he was in his teens, spoke for many of his peers:

When I first came here, I thought that life in this country would be so very different from the way it really is. This is because of the way there [El Salvador] they paint life here. There they say, "All is wonderful in the United States, everything is the best." People would say, "In the United States you can have it all." You can buy cars and all the beautiful things. There are so many commodities. So I came here with the idea of working, not going to school. I wanted to work and have it all. I thought that I would work for a few months, maybe a year, and would be rich. There [El Salvador] they exaggerate this so much.

Miguel, also from El Salvador, noted that the first thing he now tells the kids just arrived from Central America is to "forget what they think they know about life here."

Life here is not the way people in our countries say it is. There they say, "Oh, in the U.S. you can do this, in the U.S. you can buy that," without really knowing much about life here. They think everything is easy here. "You know Greens [dollars] grow on trees," they say. So the first thing I would tell them [recent arrivals] is to forget all that. I would say that if one wants to achieve something in this country one must struggle because there are real opportunities in this country, but to achieve them one must work very hard.

Reports about life in the United States, as painted mostly by people with relatives in this country and fueled by those who returned to Central America from a visit to the United States, have a magical ring to the ears of a youth. Raul, now seventeen, remembers when he first heard about the United States through the relatives of a friend who had returned to visit El Salvador.

When I first came here I was so disappointed. I had so many ideas [about life in the United States]. In El Salvador we left many big problems, my father's death and all the problems we had with the war. I had to stop studying. . . . We could not even go into the street. When I was very young, I would go out and have fun with my friends. Then the problems began. To be honest, everyone felt bad. I felt bad too. Then we decided to come here to find another system, another way of life, we wanted a different life.

When I was young, I remember the way people that went back to El Salvador from the United States would . . . bring back so much money with them! And they would tell us that life here was so different, so easy . . . to make money in the United States. Really, it is a big lie. These are the kind of people that work like slaves here, work, work, work all day, and save all the money to use in El Salvador when they go back . . . to show it off back there. They don't use any of their money here. So when I came in, I encountered all these other problems here too.

Vlach reports that Guatemalan immigrant families too had an Edenic view of the United States prior to emigrating: "All of the Guatemalan immigrants expected to find work here and better wages to support their families. In Guatemala City, information was generally available about the U.S. through newspapers, word of mouth, and television. To some, the image of the U.S. had taken on a mythic character; others simply saw it as an option to make money" (Vlach 1984: 191).

Many new immigrant youths in my sample, with their fantasies about possibilities in the affluent society, anticipated that with a little effort great fruits could be gathered. At first, some of them thought studying was not important for achieving success in the new society: life was thought to be so easy that much money could be made in a short time and without formal schooling. The inner city, however, offered most of the new arrivals a crash course in reality. A young woman from El Salvador vividly remembered her first day in the inner city: as they tried to open the door of their future home, a small apartment in a government housing project, her new neighbors showered them with rotten tomatoes from across the street.

With time the recent arrivals gained a sharper understanding of life in the inner-city barrios. The language barrier and their lack of educational credentials made their parents take whatever jobs were available. Over 80 percent of them went into service jobs—janitor and maid being the most frequently cited, with babysitting, elderly care, and restaurant work (mostly dishwasher, cook's aid, and salad person) coming next. Not one of the new arrivals in my sample received welfare. And among the recent immigrants unemployment compensation was unheard of. Far from being the easy way to "have it all," work in the new society was eventually viewed by many informants as in many respects harder than work in the country of origin. And although hourly wages were high compared to what they or their relatives made in Central America, expenses in the United States were higher too.

The new arrivals quickly became much concerned with violence in the inner city. As I was chatting with a parent one afternoon in my office, the voice of Joaquin's principal came over the loudspeakers informing us that for the fourth time a rapist had struck in the vicinity of the school, and urging all girls to go straight home after school. Many new arrivals reported being mugged by gang members hanging around the school premises. After cash, the commodity most sought after was the bus-fast-pass. A number of my informants reported having a fast-pass stolen at least once. Some informants, including girls, were brutally beaten up in the school yard. Marta, a 16-year-old from El Salvador, had a black eye for days after three large Samoan girls assaulted her in a school hall, throwing her to the floor, kicking her, and beating her up for money. Police cars were almost a permanent fixture in both schools, yet I saw ambulances only twice: both times at Joaquin High, both times after a gang fight.

As part of the inner-city pedagogical requirements, the new immigrants also had to learn to deal with drugpushers peddling their goods around the schools. One informant noted that when two youngsters approached him to buy drugs he pretended he did not understand the language. In fact, when I asked the recent arrivals to tell me the things they most disliked about their new schools, they would cite (1) racial violence (between Blacks, Filipinos, Cholos—acculturated or U.S.-born Hispanics—and Vietnamese), (2) drugs in schools, and (3) student disrespect for the teachers.

Many parents and guardians began to put restrictions on the youngsters' activities, particularly on the young women; they were not allowed to go out by themselves during the day, and to go out at night was unheard of. Thus emerges the irony that many of these families who had reported escaping political violence in Central America were being terrorized by gang and sexual violence in the inner city. Indeed, most of my female informants reported having lost some personal freedom of movement in the United States. Juana, a 14-year-old recent arrival, noted: "Here I have less freedom than in Guatemala. My grandmother is stricter with me now than she was in Guatemala. It may be because life here is so different. I had more freedom there. When I was a girl I could go out to play with my girlfriends. Here they are afraid that something would happen to me . . . that some one would hurt me." Because young women reportedly had not been sought out by the military* and the guerrillas to the same degree as the young men, most of them construed the imposition of restrictions in response to inner-city violence as a loss of personal freedom.

Some informants developed a sort of defensive armor for dealing with this situation: "be careful, do not trust people," was a common strategy. Estevan, a 17-year-old honor student from Guatemala, reports, "Here I learned that you cannot trust people. You may superficially know someone and think 'this guy is my friend,' and it turns out that he is a drugpusher or an addict. You have to be careful with your friendships." Many of them eventually took a rather instrumental attitude toward interpersonal relations with members of the host society, taking the attitude, we are immigrants here; we do not wish to change our ways; we just want to take advantage of the opportunities that exist, in order to return one day to Central America, with our hard-earned dollars. One family's action reflects the extreme of the immigrant's capacity for instrumental thinking: they sent their only daughter back to El Salvador to live with her maternal grandmother "because the morals here [in the United States] are perverse. This is not a good society in which to raise girls." Heidi, a 16-year-old from Nicaragua, agreed: "I feel that this society is more corrupt than Nicaragua. Here there are more drugs and crimes. Nicaragua is a small country and you don't see that.

* Except in Nicaragua, where the draft includes young women.

In Nicaragua people are more friendly; the people are less scared than here. Here you must always by very careful. Do your work and stay away from groups [gangs]."

The key to success for many new immigrants was simply to learn the language and to accommodate to the pace of life in the inner city, without giving up the essence of their shared code for behavior. Ana Maria, from Guatemala, said:

In this country you have more freedom to do as you please. This means that you have to be more careful in choosing your friends. My advice is to try to adapt to the pace of life here. You must learn the language without losing the basis we learn in our countries as children. The way we are taught in Guatemala is different from the way they teach here; marriage is no longer important here. Teachers in Guatemala are respected, unlike here. . . . So the bases are different.

A strategy of superficial accommodation without really giving up core cultural values is perceived as ideal. This is the Central American immigrant variant of what Gibson calls a strategy of "accommodation without assimilation" among Punjabi Sikh immigrants in California. In these cases, the immigrants see their experiences in the new land as an "additive" phenomenon: not wishing to give up their own cultural code for behavior, but readily adapting to learn the language and to acquire the behaviors and symbols seen as required for success in the host society.

Emerging Perceptions of Opportunity

As the new immigrants become more conversant with the reality of life in the inner city, they begin to abandon some of the more fantastic expectations they had carried with them on the journey north. Indeed some informants even reported seriously considering going back home as they experienced shock at the kind of life that would face them in the inner city. Herman, for example, began working for the minimum wage as a dishwasher soon after his arrival. Since he had no one to live with, he slept in an old beat-up car he bought with his first checks. A few months afterward he realized that there was no future in that kind of existence:

Then I thought of going back to El Salvador. I thought, what would I do here the rest of my life, wash dishes? Live alone in a car? So I thought it was time to go back. But the situation in El Salvador did not allow me to return. My mother did not want me to go back. She wanted to see me, but she was afraid about my safety. So I could not go back. Then I started thinking about my future. And my friend told me to enroll in school.

Herman enrolled in school, but he also continued working in restaurants.

In time, the two polarities (life as too easy and life as too hard) became overshadowed as a more balanced perception set in: though the inner city is not the rose garden they had expected, the overall situation compares favorably with life in Central America. It is precisely this comparative perspective that affords many new immigrants the capacity to endure ongoing hardships.

Ivan, a 17-year-old recent arrival from rural El Salvador, shares the advice he would give his favorite cousin from El Salvador were he to come to the inner city:

The first thing I would tell him is the things I do not like here. I would tell him all about my own experiences. I would tell him that I was assaulted by a gang, that they took my money and my bus-fast-pass, and they beat me up. I would also tell him about the things I did not like about school such as the way the students treat the teachers, without respect. But I would also tell him about the good things. About the good classes I took here, about learning English and computers. Life in the United States is not like life in El Salvador. In El Salvador you suffer . . . because life is hard. The work there is hard, it is hard to work physically. Life changes here. There you suffer day after day from 6 A.M. until 6 P.M. in the fields. The work is hard. There is suffering. And with the war things get worse every day. . . . Here there is no war, you can work and study. That is the difference.

The war and his father's illness had pushed Ivan out of elementary school in the fourth grade, to go to work the land and help feed his family.

Similarly, Estevan reflects on both the positive and the negative aspects of life in the United States:

This country is more modern than Guatemala. It has good things and it has bad things. The drugs and the fights are bad, and the welfare system is also bad. People take advantage of it, they get money without working for it. But there are opportunities to get ahead here. The government here is interested in the welfare of the people. In Guatemala, there is a lot of abuse. . . . I would not have the opportunities I now have here. I want to take full advantage of the opportunities I have here. . . . I am now learning computer programming. I could never study that in Guatemala.

Many informants see government corruption, in addition to poverty and war, as a major issue contributing to the chronic problems of Central America. Pedro commented on the differences between his native Guatemala and the United States:

Here there are more opportunities to find a good job. There we have no national funds, the national bank of Guatemala is empty. It is a big robbery. The different presidents come in saying that they want to help the country, and all they really do is take care of themselves. The people stay poor without anything. Now here you can study, you can better yourself. There are many opportunities here. I learned English here. Few people in Guatemala can learn another language. Here you can express yourself, you can complain out loud. There is no persecution like in Guatemala. There everything depends on who you know.

"Complaining out loud," or freedom of expression, in the United States was noted by many new arrivals as a key difference in the two settings.

As the reality of the inner city made its first impressions on them, many informants reported how they had felt cheated. Some had become depressed and even considered going back to Central America. Eventually, though, many informants turned to schooling as the key to a better tomorrow. Herman said, "Life here is not easy. I came in as a naïve young fellow. I sustained myself doing everything, as a dishwasher, gardener, and work like that. Then I realized that that kind of work was a dead end, that I could not better myself doing that. So, I thought, 'I have a capacity to study and if I don't exploit my brains, one day I will be sorry.'"

Schooling and the System of Status Mobility

Having identified perceptions of opportunity in the host society as a major issue in the immigrant's emerging worldview, I turned to analyzing more systematically the immigrant agenda for success in the new land. Once informants recognized that that there are more opportunities for advancement in the United States than in El Salvador, Guatemala, or Nicaragua, what specifically was the immigrants' system for status mobility (LeVine 1967)? What was their folk theory about making it in the affluent society?

As they articulated their ideas on how status mobility operated in the host society, they often paused to contrast it with the system of status mobility in the country of origin. Again, a dual frame of reference emerged in the comparison of current issues with past experiences.

Julio speaks for many:

This country gives you commodities that we cannot have in our countries. With your labor here you can have a comfortable life. There . . . you must be . . . somebody to live well. To make it there you need money and friends; friends that will introduce you to other people in good positions. Here anyone can make it, it is very different here. When the president [Ronald Reagan] spoke the other day, I heard him. And what he said is true: in this country anyone can become what he likes. He gave the example of a Vietnamese girl that came here ten years ago as a refugee. She spoke no English. Now she has graduated from the military academy [West Point] and is an officer in the U.S. Army! She really made it! But she studied and worked hard. So I agree with him. Now there is no way she would have achieved this in El Salvador!

The immigrants' contrasting perceptions of opportunity are marked. Most of them observed that whereas in the country of origin survival and success were strictly linked to prior wealth, or *por apellido* (because of your last name), and to networks of relations with people in good positions, in the United States individual effort, hard work, and study were the principal avenue to success.

As the research progressed, I became aware of how much energy the new arrivals invested in schooling and the educational system. The students in the sample were indeed thirsty for an education. Considering how uninviting both schools were, considering the patterns of gang violence, drugs, overcrowded classrooms, and burned-out teachers and counselors, and the fact that they had to learn in a new system and a new language, it seemed all the more significant that any of my informants remained in school at all.

Another key issue that pointed to the monumental importance of education was the fact that most informants faced in-

TABLE 5.1

Work Patterns of Students Attending School Full-time, by Sex and Age

(*N* = 50)

	Male/Female by Age Group				
Work Pattern	M 14–16 (*n* = 10)	F 14–16 (*n* = 10)	M 17–19 (*n* = 20)	F 17–19 (*n* = 10)	Percent of Total
Full-time	0	0	3	0	6%
Part-time	3	3	7	4	34
Full-time in the past	1	0	2	1	8
Part-time in the past	1	3	4	2	20
Never worked	5	4	4	3	32

tense pressures from their employment. The majority of the students in my sample worked, at least part time (Table 5.1). All of those who had steady jobs, and who had members of their nuclear family still in Central America, reported sending home remittances of considerable value on a regular basis. Indeed, according to Salvadorean president José Napoleón Duarte, the new arrivals who have entered the United States since 1982 have thereby contributed significantly to their native country's economy: "Between $350 million and $600 million annually, and [this amount] is thus larger than the United States Government assistance to El Salvador" (Pear 1987: 8). (For fiscal year 1984, U.S. economic aid to El Salvador totaled $329.3 million; USDS 1985). Given the opportunity, these young "Germans of Central America" (LaFeber 1984: 10) are indeed an industrious people.

During his senior year in high school Ernesto, an exceptional young man, worked full-time from 4 P.M. until after midnight as a salad boy in a restaurant. Although toward the end of his senior year this brutal pattern took its toll and he received lower grades than his usual straight A's, still he managed to graduate and eventually go on to university. Manuel worked part-time in a downtown fruit warehouse from 2 A.M. until 7 A.M. throughout his junior and senior years. Likewise, Daniel worked full-time from 6 P.M. until 2 A.M. at a restaurant and went to school at the same time. Eventually he too graduated from high school and entered a junior college. Juan, a 15-year-old from El Salvador, worked only on weekends, from 4 P.M. until 11 P.M., as a busboy in a restaurant. Some of my female informants worked as maids after school, often in the company of a relative. For example, Maria, a 16-year-old honor student from El Salvador, helped her mother clean houses. Others worked part-time and remained in school.

As many as 68 percent of my informants, both male and female, worked at some point while attending school in the United States full-time. In fact, only 30 percent in my male sample never worked while attending school full-time. This notable figure seems to tally with the HPDP's generalized finding that nationwide "Hispanic males work more hours per week while attending school than does any other [U.S.] group" (1984: 1.10).

Inasmuch as all working students reported not only that their work interfered with their schooling (see Chapter 8) but also that they had to work to help out their families, the obvious question remains: Why, given these pressures and the uninviting school atmosphere, did the new immigrants from Central America stay in school at all? The intellectual challenge is not to explain why some recent Central Americans left schools to work full-time, and some of course did, but rather why so many stayed in school. The answer leads us once again to a dual perspective in the immigrant's mind: despite the hardships it implies, schooling in the United States, unlike in the country of origin, is the key to a better tomorrow. Some parents, although eventually aware of the shortcomings of the inner-city schools, argued that schooling was nevertheless more accessible and fairer in the United States than it had been back home. They were largely unschooled or underschooled in Central America, yet they had great expectations of the American educational system. The educational system at home, particularly at the higher levels, had been closed to them. Schooling in Central America might have been better, more rigorous, and more disciplined than schooling in the inner city, yet a formal education was beyond their reach. And indeed, for periods of time during the war in El Salvador, the schools were literally closed. Let us further explore what the ethnographic record suggests in this regard.

One afternoon, in the school library, an informant, who was the father of four youngsters in the school, commented, "Look at this wonderful building," as he pointed to the seemingly endless shelves of books. "And my children can get any book they want! In El Salvador," he said, "you must buy your own text-books." Another parent expressed surprise when he found that he would not have to pay to enroll his children in school. He had assumed that foreigners would have to pay a tuition fee. He was happy to discover also that the school would lend his children the required texts for the academic year. A mother was relieved to hear that her children would again be enrolled in school at all. In her native province she had removed her three children from the school for an entire year prior to their journey North because a number of students had been assassinated. Five youths reported to me that they had been out of school in El Salvador for a period of time as a direct consequence of the war.

Some informants told me that among their friends and relatives in Central America, the pressures to leave school for full-time work were too great: "In El Salvador people cannot think of getting ahead. Some of my high-school friends had to leave school to work to help their families." Others noted that it was hard to find part-time work in Central America; joining the full-time work force almost always meant dropping out of school completely.

Most of my informants, largely from the underprivileged classes, reported that schooling in Central America was not a likely route for social mobility: "In El Salvador the only way to get ahead is if you can learn a technical skill. Maybe one in 100 gets ahead by studying. The way to get ahead in Central America is if you already have money. There are no scholarships for studying, no financial aid, unlike here." Herman echoed this theme that inequality and lack of aid in Central America made pursuing a career almost impossible:

In my country only those who have a lot of money get into the university. Even if I had graduated first in my high-school class, I could not have entered the university there. . . . To get into the university, you need more than good grades: you need the money to pay. It is very expensive to have an education, and there is no aid. Even in high school you have to pay for your own books, notebooks, everything, just like in college here. Now to enter the university a person must have parental help, or must do it on his own. . . . Not even the government gives help.

In the host society, however, perceptions change, as Julio observes:

In this country, as I see it, there are more opportunities to study. Here you can get ahead by studying. They give you aid. Here even I received aid! There if you want to study, you are on your own, you must pay your own way. The government does not even lend you the money. Look, even high school is different. I don't know how the system is in your country [Argentina], but in my country they do not give students lunch for free. Here they gave us lunch for free in the cafeteria. I see these things, and I conclude that this country offers many more opportunities.

Informants appeared to construct the system of status mobility in the new land in contrast to the system in the home country. In the United States, schooling, knowledge, and individual effort were seen as the primary avenue to mobility. On the other hand, in Central America one made it through family money, or through networks, or through nepotism, or *por apellido* (because of one's last name) and not through effort or knowledge. As one perceptive informant summarized: "There [in El Salvador] you get ahead by *who* you know; here [in the United States] you get ahead by *what* you know."

Even those who did go on to graduate from college found out that in Central America you may not be able to get ahead by what you know. Ernesto articulated the dilemma many Central Americans faced at home:

In El Salvador you can't get ahead, nobody can get ahead. You can't better yourself there. Let me give you an example. There is this man from El Salvador working in the restaurant with me. He is a dishwasher. He is about your age. He works there three times a week. One day Daniel [another new immigrant] came to me and said, "You know, our coworker José is a chemical engineer, he graduated in El Salvador two years ago!" I just sat there, my mouth dropped open. I just sat there stunned . . . "A chemical engineer!" Yes, sir, a chemical engineer working here as a dishwasher. . . . I said to myself, "How is this possible? Why did he not enter a chemical company in El Salvador? I just sat there frozen thinking about this . . . Thinking here is a man who is an engineer in my country, and *he* can't even find a job! When I asked him why he was here he said, "I couldn't get a job." That simple, he couldn't get a job!

Other informants echoed the theme that because status positions in Central America were pretty much prescribed by birth into the right family, achieving a career through individual effort and talent in the United States meant that much more. Santiago's dream was to study medicine, in part to satisfy his mother's wishes:

She wants me to be a doctor . . . a professional. She says that life here would be very different if I became a professional. She knows that in the United States the system is not like in our [Central American] countries where if you are the son of so-and-so or the son of this or that family they give you a job without asking any questions, without looking at your record. Or they leave you an inheritance, and that way you live well. Here a profession means you have done something for yourself. My mother and my father have the idea that the only thing parents leave their children is an education . . . something that nobody can take away from you. Money, on the other hand, can be taken away from you. . . . The only thing that can't be taken away from you is your knowledge, your education, your diploma.

Parents and students alike pointed to numerous features of the U.S. educational system as hard evidence of the new opportunities in the host society: the schools are open and free, even to foreigners; the texts are given to children for the entire year for free; many students received a free hot lunch in the school cafeteria; and there were special programs such as bilingual classes, classes in ESL, classes on computers, and so forth. These positive considerations frequently seemed to overshadow the obvious negative aspects of schooling in the inner city—the violence, lack of discipline and respect, filth, outdated materials, and the like—that the teachers, mostly American-born and lacking the comparative perspective of the new immigrants, emphasized.

In the opinion of informants, a harsh system of inequality in Central America was at the root of why birth into the right family had a larger influence in determining status than did individual effort or talent. Most informants had only to look at their parents to see how difficult it was to complete an education. On the other hand, the educational system of the host society, faulty as it was, offered them the chance to become somebody. A dual frame of reference, comparing present and prior realities, emerges as the matrix in which the new immigrants evaluated ongoing experiences and planned for the future. In thinking about the meaning of schooling and the future, they would pause and make comparative statements between the "here" and the "there." The key issues that surfaced to immunize the new immigrants to endure hardships in the inner city were a belief that no matter how bad things seemed to be in the inner city, they were never as bad as they would be at home; and anticipation of a better tomorrow through hard work and study in their new land of opportunity.

SIX

"Becoming Somebody": The Anatomy of Achievement Among New Immigrant Hispanics

IN LATE NOVEMBER 1984, almost four years after escaping El Salvador, Ernesto took a group of his high-school classmates to visit the campus of a nearby university. He organized the entire affair: he contacted the university and arranged to have a bilingual counselor meet the group of Hispanic students and take them around campus and tell them about the facilities, programs, and opportunities; he requested a bus from the school district; he prepared and sent out the parent/guardian consent forms; and, as required, he arranged for a teacher to go with them. The excursion was such a success that Ernesto took groups of his Spanish-speaking classmates to visit other colleges twice again that academic year.

On the surface, this incident does not seem particularly out of the ordinary. Upon closer scrutiny, however, it is paradigmatic of an immigrant involutional achievement syndrome: estimates that the new arrivals send between $350 million to $600 million annually to El Salvador (Pear 1987: 8) underscore the fact that they are here to work, to work hard and "to become somebody." Ernesto's parents had not completed an elementary education. At the time of the research reported here, he lived alone in the inner city, and in addition to studying full-time and being an honor student, he worked 40 hours a week in a local restaurant. In brief, had anyone tried to forecast what a 15-year-old, working-class, monolingual Spanish-speaking boy from war-torn El Salvador would end up doing four years later in a run-down American inner city, living alone, few would have guessed that he would be working at night to support himself and to send money home to his parents, and taking his peers to universities around the area to show them the educational opportunities available to them in the host society.

What he accomplished was in fact not so extraordinary among the immigrants in this study. Daniel also worked full-time at night, was also an honor student, and tutored younger new immigrants in his favorite subject—algebra—during his lunch hour. When Daniel graduated from high school, he went on to a junior college. Angel, the son of a Salvadorean maid, also graduated from high school and went on to enroll at a prestigious U.S. university. Manuel, from Guatemala, was a full-time student and worked every morning from 2 A.M. until 7 A.M. at a large downtown market to help his mother and father pay the bills. Yet, he managed to stay on the honor roll throughout his high-school years.

Pedro, José, and Maria were also honor students, and while Maria worked only at home (de facto, she ran the household), the boys worked every morning before school to help their mother financially. In fact, although 68 percent of my informants worked while attending high school full-time at one point or another, close to 50 percent of them were honor-roll students sometime during their high-school career. And five of the newly arrived graduating seniors in my sample (10 percent of the entire sample) went on to enroll at U.S. universities.

Vlach found that, of the five recent immigrant Guatemalan families she studied, four scored well above average in achievement themes in the Family Environment Scale, a tool used to "describe and measure family environments with respect to interpersonal relationships, personal growth, and organizational structure" (Vlach 1984: 38). In particular, the adolescents in the immigrant families now residing in a U.S. inner city seem motivated to study. Although these families report a number of the same problems I encountered, the children do well in school, seemingly against all odds. A sample of Vlach's findings:

[The Walter family] are pleased with the schools for their younger girls, but Laura's middle school worries them. They feel that there is too much drug-taking, loose morality, and not enough control of the behavior of these adolescents. They also feel that the work is too easy for Laura. She is doing extremely well and has even been moved up a grade so that she (at 12) is in classes with primarily 13 and 14 year olds. The parents feel that Guatemalan education is definitely superior to what they have found here. [Vlach 1984: 64–65]

Of another family, she writes:

Ernesto is in the ninth grade in a large urban high school. He started out attending a special high school designed for immigrant students, but was transferred to the school he now attends after a semester. In addition to his studies, Ernesto also works as a dishwasher in a restaurant five days a week, six hours a day. Ernesto says he is doing well, having no problems [in school], but he is bewildered by the great numbers of students who cut classes and do not seem to take their studies seriously. Ernesto has to bus across town to get to school, but he does not see this as a hardship as he had to walk long distances to school in Guatemala. He is getting "good marks" in mathematics and art. English is his biggest problem. Having been in the United States less than a year, he feels that once he learns English, everything else will follow. Ernesto has ambitions to be a medical doctor. [Vlach 1984: 106]

Vlach goes on to note that Ernesto is the pride of his family. And in the "Navarro family,"

School is a topic of much interest to the entire family. . . . All three members of the family are in school. Mrs. Navarro and Hugo study at night in adult school English classes. They go four nights a week. Gordon is a scholarship student who has been singled out by his teachers and counselors as having great potential. His mother is quite proud of his scholastic achievements which include a number of certificates and prizes for attendance, good citizenship, and a scholarship to go to a backpacking camp in Yosemite through the Police Athletic league. He gets excellent grades, and his mother says the schoolwork is easy for him since school in the U.S. is much easier than it is in Guatemala. [Vlach 1984: 154]

We have observed that perceptions of parental sacrifice and of opportunity help create the certainty in the immigrants' minds that in the long run their efforts will be rewarded. We have noted how the recent arrivals come to view formal education as the choice system for status mobility. There is nothing cultural per se in the veneration for education and formal schooling. In Central America schooling was simply not a viable system for mobility, certainly not at the lower levels of the socioeconomic hierarchy. Notions about investing in education as the system of mobility developed as the immigrants settled in the new land and began to explore ways to make it. The new immigrants' attraction to the educational system is closely related to a specific process of resettling in a new sociocultural atmosphere. As such, the psychosocial motivational dynamics analyzed here best describe the experiences of a cohort of new arrivals who escaped under circumstances that were unique. Other cohorts of immigrants, who had not escaped a situation of war or left relatives behind in economic scarcity and political terror, would hardly exhibit the same psychosocial motivational concerns and dynamics.

In order to assess the seemingly unshakable determination of my informants to achieve a better tomorrow, and to analyze the anatomy of the achievement-nurturance cluster, I shall examine their responses to Cards 1 and 2, respectively, of the TAT.

Achievement, Adequacy, and Dependency

Card 1 portrays a young boy contemplating a violin that rests on a table in front of him (see Fig. 1). The stories in my sample of new arrivals attest to comparatively high achievement motivation.* Of the stories I collected, 56 percent picture the boy as working hard to achieve mastery over the violin. This is as high a figure as De Vos noted in other high-achievement groups such as Japanese-Americans and Korean immigrants (1973, 1983a; see Table 6.1).† The TAT would simply be a waste of time if it only confirmed what was obvious to the anthropologist and the teachers who came into daily contact with the new arrivals: that they were highly motivated. The intricate subtleties that compose the new immigrant's motivations emerge, however, when the TAT stories are scored.

---

* I use the term *achievement motivation* following McClelland et al. 1953: 161 and LeVine 1967: 100–102 in their use of the term as a "competition with a standard of excellence."

† De Vos (1983a: 29) gives the following figures for responses indicating self-initiated achievement (all his respondents were U.S. residents): Koreans 52 percent; first-generation Japanese 93 percent; second-generation Japanese 57 percent; middle-class Whites 67 percent; lower-class Whites 35 percent.

FIG. 1. Adapted Thematic Apperception Test Card 1

Card 1 elicited a thematic cluster intertwining three distinct phenomena: (1) issues of achievement in relation to a dependence on others for assistance or help, or in the context of helping others, that is, achievement-nurturance; (2) issues of achievement permeated with questions about adequacy, or achievement-adequacy; and (3) issues of motivational ambivalence.

In only 4 percent of the Central American narratives are there themes of individualistic achievement; such themes are more characteristic of middle-class Americans, immigrant Koreans, and Japanese. In 8 percent of the Central American stories the boy is simply daydreaming that he will one day become a great musician.

The achievement-nurturance cluster surfaced rather strongly in both Card 1 and Card 2 of the TAT. In the former, the boy achieves mastery only after an adult, his father perhaps, or his older brother or a grandfather, gives him the violin, helps him, or gives him lessons. Nurturance in this case is an act of giving in a vertical relationship. Accomplishment is conceived of in a nurturant context with members of an older generation; in this case it is not individualistically oriented, nor is it peer-oriented. Here, in summary form, is a sampling of relevant stories:

The boy did not know how to play the violin. He looks for an older man to teach him. He finds help. He practices the violin and eventually gets ahead in life by playing the violin. He then teaches other children to play.

He is bored, He would love to play the violin. An older friend takes him to school with him. The older friend teaches him. They study hard together. After some time he becomes a star.

He seeks help with the violin. Someone helps him play it. He learns how to play the violin well.

In other cases the boy wants to be able to nurture others, most commonly family members perceived to be enduring hardships:

This is a boy from a very poor family. He thinks a great deal about his poor family. He thinks that playing the violin will bring his family many benefits. He thinks about his younger siblings, he wants to be an example to them. He will become an example to all. He will play the violin very well to make money to help his family. In the future the violin will help them a great deal.

TABLE 6.1

Summary of Central American Immigrants' Responses to TAT Card 1, by Sex and Age

$(N = 50)$

Theme	Male/Female by Age Group				Percent of Total Responses
	M 14–16 ($n = 10$)	F 14–16 ($n = 10$)	M 17–19 ($n = 20$)	F 17–19 ($n = 10$)	
Self-initiated achievement	1	0	0	1	4%
Motivational ambivalence	0	1	2	2	10
Parental pressure	0	1	0	0	2
Achievement-adequacy	4	2	5	4	30
Achievement-nurturance	2	4	9	3	36
Passive about achievement	2	0	2	0	8
Pleasure	0	0	2	0	4
Other	1	1	0	0	4
Rejected card	0	1	0	0	2

These narratives capture an ethos of mutual nurturance and cooperation: the boy is able to achieve only after recruiting the benevolent aid of a nurturing older figure, or, conversely, achieving becomes a way to ease parental poverty or economic concerns. In this world, "a somebody" helps take care of his people; he or she reciprocates.

In another common thematic cluster, achievement-adequacy, a doubt about adequacy emerges rather strongly: at first the boy lacks the ability to play the violin and eventually, through hard work and study, he overcomes the initial barrier:

The boy is interested in the violin but does not have the ability to play. He really wanted to play. He makes great efforts and after a long time he is successful.

The boy cannot play the violin. He wishes to play. He studies hard and becomes a famous violinist.

The boy has been practicing the violin for hours. He could not play as well as he wished. He then puts more effort. He continues to play with great desire.

In a few stories, however, he is incapable of overcoming his inadequacy: "He leaves the violin on the table thinking 'I can't play it; I better leave it here.'"

Perhaps the most striking feature of the narratives on Card 1 is the frequency with which an older figure is invoked as a source of nurturance: in 32 percent of the stories the boy achieves success because (1) others help him, or (2) inspire him, or because (3) he achieves with the help of others and then turns to help yet others, or (4) his parents give him lessons, or (5) he simply achieves to help others. In 4 percent of the stories the boy is desperate because he cannot find anyone to help him with the task. In very few stories, however, is a parental figure pictured as imposing the task on the boy. In fact, a statistically remarkable fact about this sample is the low frequency in which a parental figure is seen as assigning the task of playing the violin to the child. The fact that in only one narrative to Card 1 is a parental figure depicted as making the child play the violin is significant when compared with other populations. De Vos cites examples from Caudill's sample of working-class white North Americans (1973: 231; 1983a: 29). In 65 percent of these stories a parental figure is prodding the boy to play. De Vos (1973: 232) reports some typical stories, presented here in summary form:

Doesn't want to play his violin. Hates his music lessons. His mother wants him to be a musician, but he's thinking about breaking the violin. He is not thinking about the music. He is thinking about a swimming hole. When his mother quits pushing the violin on him, he will break away from it altogether.

Banfield (1958: 185–86) too reports the following typical responses to Card 1 from rural Kansas, in summary:

It looks to me like a little kid's got to take violin lessons. . . . He seems pretty bored. . . . He's dreaming about what some other kids outside—maybe there's a good ball game going on, I don't know. His mother probably wants him to be a great concert violinist someday, but he seems pretty bored. He turns out to be a big league ball player.

He is looking at his violin. He's probably been told to practice his violin. He will make up his mind to play the violin and become a great artist.

He is tired of practicing his lesson. While he thinks about doing something ouside, his mother probably tells him to get back to practicing so he probably does. He becomes quite accomplished and plays in an orchestra.

In these North American stories, regardless of whether the *dramatis persona* achieves success with the violin, a major thematic concern is whether the boy *wants* to play the violin, not whether he will be *able* to play it, as is the case in my new-immigrant sample. In the Central American sample, adequacy is a major concern in relation to achievement. In the North American stories the parental figures, which incidentally are not visually present in Card 1, are introduced as setting the task for the boy. Here the psychological issue is not self-motivated, internalized behavior coupled with concerns over adequacy—the boy wants to play the violin, and the question is, can he?—but rather the absence of any desire to play. Among the Central Americans motivational ambivalence is present in only five stories, 10 percent of the sample. In the Central American sample, the striking issue is how often the child himself is seen as trying to recruit the help of an older figure.

In brief, the two themes that recur significantly in the Central

American immigrant narratives are (1) Will the boy be able to overcome an initial inadequacy while facing the difficult task of mastering the violin? And (2) will he receive or recruit the help of a nurturing older figure to accomplish the difficult goal of learning the violin? These thematic concerns are isomorphic to certain fundamental issues in the life of the new immigrants in the host society.

The recent arrivals find themselves in a new land, operating in a new cultural environment, desperately trying to learn a new language while at the same time working to help support their families. The implicit difficulties seem sometimes insuperable. Among most of my informants, even the most brilliant and self-assured had doubts at some point about this magnificent feat— the search for peace and opportunity. One informant reported a shared concern:

When we come here from Central America, we are afraid. We are even afraid of talking to people with the little English we speak. . . . At first I was so timid. I could not even engage in a conversation. I was afraid people would laugh at my English. We are afraid of this so we shut our-selves in our little universe thinking, how will we get ahead in this country, not even speaking the language? . . . Look at Daniel, my best friend, he was afraid to go talk to the counselor about changing some of his classes. He always would ask me to go with him because he was afraid she would not understand him. This is the way we are; we are afraid of others.

Other informants reported feeling intense anxiety because they did not know how to act in the new land. A recent immigrant from El Salvador reported engaging in the following strategy:

When I came here, I noticed how different people are [from Salvador-eans]. Here they dress differently, they talk differently, they act differ-ently. I did not know how to act here, I did not know how to speak English, I did not know what to do or what to say. So the first thing I did was to try to dress like everybody else. I did not want to stand out. Because people here notice if you are dressed very differently. They may not say anything directly to you, but they do notice. . . . I did not want to look like a stranger, I did not want to stand out. The next thing I did was to pay attention to what people here did, how they spoke and how they acted. I tried to learn how and why they acted in a certain way because I didn't know.

In fact, the new immigrants reported almost universally that entering this society from Central America was such a tremendous change that, even beyond the natural course of "culture shock," they often felt quite self-conscious of the "backward" ways in their countries. A 17-year-old new immigrant from El Salvador commented:

Life in my country is very backward. There we live in a humble way. You are remote from everything. The people are ignorant. You can't do anything there, you can't travel, you can't learn another language. . . . Here people are open and there is freedom, here there are people from all over the world. This is a liberal country. This is the most modern country in the world. There the kids grow up in the shadows of their mothers' skirts. They train you to be obedient.

Here I don't see that. . . . This is another world. Here you have the freedom to do whatever pleases you. Here there are opportunities that we do not have in El Salvador. . . . This is why when Salvadorans get here they do not know how to act.

Resettling in the most modern country in the world without knowledge of the language, the code of behavior, or a wide array of other new cultural symbols evokes a sense of inadequacy in the immigrants as they face the task of survival. This anxiety over not knowing how to act in the new land is reflected in the narratives to Card 1 of the TAT.

Solitude and the Search for a Parent

The second major thematic cluster in Card 1 is that of achievement via nurturance, which is also significant because it reappears as the primary narrative in Card 2. The search for a helpful adult may be related to two key issues: (1) only a small minority of the new immigrants lived in the host society with both parents (see Table 6.2); and (2) among those living with one or both parents, the youngster's insight was that, once settled in the new land, parents in a certain sense are no longer there as they had been in the past, or would be had they all remained at home. In a sense, the migration process made many of my informants feel like orphans even while their parents were still alive.

Of my informants, 62 percent had one or both parents still residing in a war-torn Central American country; the parents of

TABLE 6.2

Residence of Members of the Nuclear Family

(N = 50)

Location	Country of Origin			Percent of Total
	El Salvador (n = 33)	Nicaragua (n = 8)	Guatemala (n = 9)	
In country of origin				
Both parents and one or more sibs	4	3	0	14%
One parent and one or more sibs	10	0	2	24
One parent	6	3	3	24
One or more sibs	1	0	0	2
In a third country				
One or both parents	1	0	0	2
With informant in U.S.				
Both parents and all sibs	9	2	4	30
One parent (other parent deceased) and all sibs	2	0	0	4

one resided in a third country. This fact seemed to generate two basic concerns. First, most informants remained anxious about *la situación* in Central America. This basic fact became an intricate part of their dream: to work hard to be able to help get their loved ones out. Second, a strong sense of solitude descended upon many informants as they began to emerge from the initial shock of resettlement.

Alberto, an 18-year-old, had left both parents and four siblings in El Salvador. He shared a small studio with an older Salvadorean couple and paid them a portion of the rent and for his own food and expenses. He had a half-brother living in the United States, about three hours away by car, but they saw one another less than a dozen times during his four years of residency in the United States. Alberto reflected on the brutal sense of solitude that sometimes engulfed him:

Here I have no family, I have no home. If I had my family and a home here I would be more optimistic. Now I feel tired. . . . I am sure that if I had a home here, my mother would be waiting for me with my food ready. Now I come back home, and I have to make my food. I get up in the morning to go to school, and I am all by myself. I make my own coffee, iron my clothes, do everything alone. I come back from work at night and I am all alone. I feel very low. I sit in bed all alone, and I lose morale. I think about my future and about being all alone. This depresses me a lot; I feel desperate.

In the TAT stories in which the search for the older character is successful, that is, in which the boy recruits help and achieves his dream of mastering the violin, we see the fulfillment, albeit in fantasy, of a dear wish: to have a nurturing parent close by in the struggle to succeed.

Among many informants the sense of solitude is overwhelming, as the following story conveys in moving fashion:

This is a boy with a violin. . . . He is studying to learn to play the musical instrument. He feels desperate because he has no one to help him, no one to teach him the first steps in music. He is alone in this world, and he has a wish to get ahead with his instrument. . . . He wishes to learn to play melodies. He wishes to play the violin very well. He wishes to take advantage of the violin, and to treat the violin with care.

The lonely boy is doing the best he can to play beautiful music, this is what comes from his heart, to better himself in music, which is what he wants to do. But now he is desperate because there is no one to help him.

He, all alone, has set the objective to learn to play the violin.

This is not to suggest that the sense of solitude is related to a clear-cut generational conflict that alienates the youngsters from the parents. In fact, those who could, did search out their parents for advice and guidance, as appears in the TAT responses. In response to Card 7BM, for example, in which a gray-haired man is looking at a younger man who is staring sullenly into space, most of my informants pictured the younger fellow as seeking advice from a benevolent parental figure, or the parental character as giving advice or guidance to the younger fellow (in 48 percent of all stories, $N = 50$).

The new arrivals lucky enough to have even one parent residing with them were far from alienated from the older generation, but they did have to work through the fact that their parents were no longer parents in the full sense of the term. In the new context the older generation faced severe handicaps: most of them knew less English than their children did; their jobs in the inner city were less satisfying than the ones they had anticipated; they suffered from a feeling of frustration because they could not help their children with even the most basic school issues. Indeed, parents and guardians felt quite helpless not knowing the language and increasingly relied on their children to translate for them in job interviews, to fill out forms, set up bank accounts, pay bills, and so forth. In the context of resettling the youth often became, in a sense, the parents' cultural parents. The search for a competent, nurturing parental figure in Card 1 of the TAT may be seen as the fulfillment of a wish in fantasy.

In the course of documenting the presence of a rather marked achievement motive among the new immigrants, I have consciously avoided entering the heated debate over measuring achievement more objectively—by means of scholastic achievement tests, for example, or the Stanford Diagnostic Reading and Writing Tests, or even IQ tests—for a variety of reasons. First and foremost, these "objective" tests, standardized on a White Anglo-Saxon North American population, would be hopelessly unfair to the new arrivals unfamiliar with the linguistic and cultural nuances deemed worthy of measurement by test-developers. Second, most of these tests are in multiple-choice format, a testing approach familiar to native North Americans, but largely foreign to the new arrivals. Finally, these tests operate within a rigidly fixed time-frame, another variable foreign to the new arrivals, who were used to being tested at length, either orally or in writing, in their Central American schools, with time seldom intervening as a variable.

The TAT, even with its shortcomings (see Lindzey 1961; Henry 1956), avoided some of these issues. It was given after six months of preliminary ethnographic work and only after I had gained the trust of many informants. No one individual was forced to take the test, and in fact a number of new immigrants volunteered. All stories were collected in Spanish, and without any time pressures. Informants were allowed to go on for as long as they wished. I also made it clear that there was "no right or wrong answer," and that my informants were not being tested for a grade, but rather that I wished to explore how they constructed narratives.

Analysis of the responses to TAT Card 1 gives a subtle insight into the micro-anatomy of the new immigrants' strong desire to succeed, to overcome obstacles through hard work. Dissecting their achievement motivation revealed a recurring uncertainty about adequacy, which was eventually overcome through hard work in many instances. I interpret this sense of inadequacy as isomorphic to the fears and anxieties many new immigrants feel as they settle in the foreign land. In the other major thematic cluster that surfaced, the achievement motive is intertwined with a search for a nurturing older figure to help master the task at hand.

In sharp contrast to the U.S. achievement syndrome, with its individualistic concern for self-advancement and independence, are the readings from the Card 2 narratives, in which achieving is based on a wish to help others, most often less fortunate relatives in need. This is explored in the next chapter.

SEVEN

Nurturance and the Pursuit of a Dream

MANY PARENTS came to endure the resettlement process as a function of what the future would bring their children. During our interviews they stated explicitly that they had come to the United States so the children could find peace and make a better tomorrow in the new land. There were other parents who had the resources to send only one of their children out of the engulfing Central America war. The youths whom I came to know were keenly aware of what had happened and what was still happening there. Among some informants, particularly those with close relatives remaining behind, something akin to survivor guilt has appeared (Bettelheim 1980: 274–314). The syndrome is similar in some aspects to the guilt felt by survivors of the Nazi death machine: a sense that one's life was spared only because someone else had suffered or died. The concept of "limited good" that Foster describes in the context of economic behavior in Latin American peasant societies (1967: 300–23) is manifested to some degree by my informants in their thinking about their own and their families' survival vis-à-vis the often inexplicable death of others.

Many immigrant youths live with the conscious knowledge that they were sent out of Central America whereas loved ones, including siblings and parents, had to remain behind. Table 6.2 reveals that 64 percent of my informants had at least one member of their nuclear family still residing in Central America—not counting more distant relatives and friends. Among the youth the sense of desperation that ensues becomes the focus in a plan to rescue others and to alleviate the ongoing hardships of those responsible for sending them out toward freedom. To survive meant living with the certainty that one had to survive "for a purpose" (Bettelheim 1980: 393). The importance of being somebody is then related to a survivor's teleology; namely, to help alleviate the continuous suffering of loved ones left behind. Young Herman summarized: "Now there are three important things for me to do in the future. First, to continue studying for a career, second to get the residency papers in order to have a better life in this country, and once I have a career and my papers I will bring my family to safety."

There are both "instrumental" and "expressive" components inherent in this plan. Viewed instrumentally, achieving status and wealth is a purpose for many immigrants. Among my informants, however, this behavior was almost never entertained in individualistic terms. Rather, achievements were seen as expressive of feelings of love and of a need for care and closeness. On the expressive level, the new immigrant's activities in the host society are related to a belief that achieving would symbolically mean finally making the parents' sacrifices worthwhile. Indeed, a number of the youngsters reported that the single most important thing they could do for their parents was to become *universitario* (professional), because of the pride and satisfaction this would afford their parents. Achievement through education, in and of itself, becomes a tribute to one's parents. As Angel put it: "I believe the most important thing I can do for my parents is to become a doctor; that would make them happy. I will be the first professional in my family. . . . She [mother] does not want me to lead a life such as they had to live when they were young. They had a hard life. They had to work hard, sacrifice themselves." Indeed, more than once I heard the statement "They [the parents] want me to be what they could not be" from the lips of informants.

The feeling of guilt that motivates the new immigrants arises in the context of a specific interpersonal morality. Any system of morality is rooted in the awareness that action and thought may have positive or negative consequences for other individuals. Developmentally, human beings become increasingly more aware of their own capacity to hurt or help others by deeds committed or omitted (Piaget 1930). In a normally adjusted person, the awareness that one's behavior may create pain in others makes one prone to feelings of guilt. Among the new immigrants from Central America guilt feelings derive from an insight (1) that loved ones have sacrificed heavily in securing their well-being and (2) that they have been selected above others to enjoy the relative security and opportunities of the new environment. Such awareness creates a ready propensity to intense guilt, should they fail or become derelict in their social duties. These feelings, if they occur, can be assuaged only by expiatory re-application to the task at hand. Feelings of desperation give way to a harsh sense of responsibility that drives them to seize upon any opportunities. Achieving in school and working to ease parental hardships are intimately related to this psychosocial syndrome of proneness to guilt over one's selective survival.

It is very hard for even the most insightful individual to articulate with ease the feelings and thoughts related to this emotion–laden syndrome. Most informants would only say, "I feel bad that my brother is still in El Salvador, he may be drafted any day, I am trying to help him get out." Or, "it bothers me that my mother kills herself cleaning houses so I can study," and so forth. Although I began over time to sense the recurring nature of this basic concern, it was my informants' responses to the TAT, particularly to Card 2, that more fully sensitized me to the subtle dynamics at work. Their responses to the TAT captured a subtle cluster of interpersonal concerns that I had sensed during the course of fieldwork, but could not explore so directly with them. We could converse more comfortably about other issues, such as the nature of the opportunity structure in Central America or schooling in the United States as the key system for status mobility.

The new immigrants were being motivated to achieve out of a newly emerging ethic that through hard work and study they could position themselves in a more advantageous role to help relatives and others. As a young man from El Salvador put it: "Studying is the most important thing I can now do. Graduating [from college] will bring my parents the satisfaction that I have become somebody, I will be a professional . . . the first professional in my family. And that is what my parents want. They could not go to school. I have a chance now to make up for their deprivations by becoming a professional." Far from being related to a wish for independence or individual self-advancement, the new immigrant's plans are intricately related to a profound desire to rescue others.

The Underlying Grammar of Achievement and Help

Card 2 of the TAT is a country scene (see Fig. 2). "In the foreground is a young woman with books in her hand; in the background a man is working in the fields and an older woman is looking on" (Murray 1943: 18). The new arrivals usually interpreted this card as depicting a family group enduring hardships and economic deprivation, the parental figures sacrificing, often to send the young woman to school. The young woman studies hard to avoid repeating her parents' cycle of hard work and scarcity and eventually achieves high status and becomes somebody. Finally, and of critical importance to understanding the psychosocial profile of the new arrivals, rather than leaving her parents behind, as in the stories told by independent and individualistic North Americans (De Vos 1983), the protagonist of these immigrant Hispanic stories returns home to take care of her poor parents and to end their hardship by her own work.

FIG. 2. Adapted Thematic Apperception Test Card 2

Here are a number of representative stories for Card 2, in summary form:

Her parents were poor. Peasants have few opportunities to study. But her parents did all they could to send her to study. They bought her books and paid for her schooling. At the end she was well prepared and worked hard to help her parents get out of the hard work they endured all their lives. She betters their way of life.

She has books. Her parents work the land. She wants to study to become somebody. She wants a career. Her parents are very poor. She wants a career to help her poor parents, so they do not have to suffer so much. She studies hard and becomes somebody. Her parents are so proud of her. With their help she is able to become a professional. Whenever they need help, she is there for them.

She is looking at her poor parents working hard on the land so she can study, so she can become somebody. She wants to achieve something so that her parents do not continue to live in poverty, always working so hard. The mother is thinking that one day her daughter will do something for them. And that is why they give her the possibility to study. They work hard so that in the future their daughter may become someone, so she won't have to live through what they had to live through. The daughter will get them out of poverty. She will get them out of their misery. She will study hard, she will become a good, educated person. She goes to school to become somebody.

A father, daughter, and the mother. The mother is pregnant. The man is struggling so that his daughter can get ahead studying. This gives her a desire to continue studying. She dedicates herself to studying. She will win; she will get ahead. That way she shall pay back her parents for their sacrifice. She continues studying hard and is able to get her parents out of poverty.

She is the daughter of hard-working peasants. They sent her to school. She loved school. She did very well in school. She worked very hard in school to be able to get her family out of poverty. She became an important, educated, and outstanding person. She helped her family. She placed her family in a better environment.

Table 7.1 summarizes the major thematic clusters emerging in the stories told by the new immigrants. In 50 percent of the stories in this sample the heroine achieves success in school and then turns to help her folks. And in one story the girl just remains on the farm to help her parents; there is no mention

TABLE 7.1

Summary of Central American Immigrants' Responses to TAT Card 2,
by Sex and Age

(N = 50)

| Theme | Male/Female by Age Group | | | | Percent of Total Responses |
	M 14–16 (n = 10)	F 14–16 (n = 10)	M 17–19 (n = 20)	F 17–19 (n = 10)	
Nurturance	5	3	16	4	56%
Independence	2	2	1	3	16
Family harmony	2	2	1	0	10
Suffering	0	0	0	2	4
Mutuality	0	0	2	0	4
Other	1	1	0	1	6
Rejected card	0	2	0	0	4

of school success. In the greatest number of stories education emerges as the most likely avenue for helping parents, which supplements the view of it as the mode for status mobility (Chapter 6).

Dissecting the underlying structural narrative sequence, we find a pattern in the stories: (1) the heroine perceives the parental figures working hard, suffering, (2) often for the purpose of providing her an education; (3) she makes up her mind that studying is the most efficient mode to help them; (4) she studies hard and eventually becomes somebody; at that point (5) she returns to her parents, to ease their hardships. The incidence of this thematic cluster is interesting and revealing from a comparative perspective. De Vos (1983a: 25–71), for example, found that in similar stories among Korean immigrants in the Los Angeles area, there was a related theme that self-consciously examined ambivalence about maintaining traditional Confucian family roles and discharging one's duty to family members (in 30 percent of his sample). In the Korean stories, poverty did not emerge as a key issue. The idea of rescuing sacrificing parents through studying appeared in only 10 percent of the immigrant Korean sample (see De Vos 1983a: 37), which contrasts sharply with the Central American case. Clearly these two immigrant populations have very different interpersonal concerns, although both evidence a strong concern with achievement. The theme of personal ambition combined with a wish for independence from the parental figures appears in 16 percent of the stories in the Central American sample—and, incidentally, in 30 percent of the White middle-class North American sample (see De Vos 1983*a*). In only three stories told by immigrant Central Americans does the young woman leave her parents behind because she does not wish to lead the kind of life they live. In those stories, the young woman does not return to help the parental figures. One story is essentially a righteous statement about achievement: the young woman is pictured as happy, with a confident smile on her face "because she studied hard," and the poor peasants are viewed as having to slave because "they did not study."

Of the Central American stories for Card 2, 10 percent are characterized by themes of family harmony and affiliation, with all characters dutifully discharging their roles. In two stories (4 percent of the sample) the young woman is depicted as being sad, and in two others as being a teacher who is engaged in a mutually beneficial relationship with the farmers. The young woman is teaching illiterate farmers to read and write, and they are teaching her solid "farmers' values" in one case, and "about life" in general, in the other.*

The theme of desperation over the lack of a helping, nurturing figure on whom to depend for help also appeared in narratives to Card 2. In two stories the young woman wishes to go to school but feels desperate because her parents are too poor to send her to school, or she just has no help in the pursuit of her studies. In one story, the parents are too poor to send her to school, so the heroine goes into farming to alleviate their burden. There were, in addition, three essentially unimaginative descriptions of the card, and two rejections of it—both by young women.

Seventy percent (14 out of 20) of the young men aged 17 to 19 years old articulated narratives that climaxed when the heroine turned to help her parents. This may be related to the ethnographic fact that it was the older, more mature students who seemed most concerned about their parents' sacrifices. In Table

---

* One of the informants who produced such a story had himself spent time teaching illiterate farmers in rural Nicaragua during the Sandinista drive to teach the rural population to read and write.

5.1, one may note that in the same 17–19 age category, only 4 of 20 males had never worked while attending school in the United States. The dream to end parental suffering was most evident among these older, more responsible informants. They were also the ones often pointed out by teachers as being the most motivated to learn English.

The TAT materials, in my opinion, captured the essence of the new immigrants' project in the host land: to work hard toward achieving the status that would enable them to take care of others, a theme that surfaced repeatedly in the immigrants' responses to other TAT cards. A narrative to Card 13B—a little boy is sitting on the doorstep of a log cabin—crystalizes around this basic interpersonal concern common to most new immigrants:

A boy is in his wooden house. He is watching his father work on the farm . . . how hard his father works to feed him and his mother. He thinks that when he grows up he will be able to help his father, so as to make his father's work easier, his life less hard. He . . . will plant the seeds for a better tomorrow. One day he will harvest a good career. Then he will do . . . his best to help his family move to a better place. They lived all their lives in a poor country and they are ready for a change.

Why should a picture of a little boy sitting on a doorstep conjure up a hard-working father in a poor country? There is no such parental figure depicted on the card. Structurally, this story is another version of the type isolated in analyzing responses to Card 2: deprivation, compensatory achievement, and, finally, nurturance. This shared concern among the new immigrants is quite eloquent. The hero is affected by the realization that the parental characters sacrifice a great deal on his behalf. This insight mobilizes his energy toward achieving "somebody" status, by means of formal education, schooling, or a career. Last, and perhaps most important, the hero almost predictably returns to his folks to expiate past as well as ongoing sacrifices.

The following story, also a response to TAT Card 13B, reveals essentially the same concern, emphasizing the role of schooling in the hero's project:

This is about a boy, Rodolfo. He lives in a barrio outside the city. He is a poor boy, from a very poor family. So he had to work since he was young. By the time he was five he worked and lived in the streets.

His mother is sick. And his father left her when Rodolfo was born. He has to work shining shoes and selling candies. Sometimes he even works at night to earn enough to have a tortilla to eat.

One day the boy began thinking about the future. Will he be a good man? Or, will he be a bad man? He also thinks about school and the streets. And about the differences that exist between the two. After thinking about all this he discovered that there was a great difference between the street and school: that difference is knowledge, the capacity to know what is good and what is bad.

After meditating about this, Rodolfo told his mother that he was going to do his best to continue in school. He told his sick mother not to worry about anything because he would also work. He would work and study . . . no matter how hard it was to do both, or how much he would suffer.

This is exactly what Rodolfo did. Years later he was a model student in school. After finishing high school, he went to the university to study law. He chose law because he thought that it would be the best way to help as many poor children as possible.

The emerging pattern is isomorphic to previous narratives: a boy from an economically deprived home perceives that education is the route out of misery. By systematic, self-sacrificing work and study, the hero becomes an attorney. He studies and works so that his poor, sick mother would not worry. At the end, his achievement is translated into helping as many poor youngsters as possible. The climax is not individualistic self-indulgence, but rather the conversion of success into concrete help for needy people. This, I argue, is the underlying grammar of the program of immigrant youths in the affluent society.

Next, I consider the improbability of alternative routes for mobility, particularly the achievement-independence variant and the achievement-passing variant, as viable strategies in the new land.

Leaving Home and Its Discontents

In only a few stories for Card 2 did the theme of independence occur. The heroine goes off to study in a distant city and becomes successful. Never again do we hear about the parental figures, which may not be surprising. Indeed, some may argue that this is the standard pattern among upwardly mobile lower-status and ethnic individuals, for whom "making it" has implied, particularly in the United States, breaking away from the older generation and leaving them behind in the search for a modern identity in the affluent society. In Scott Fitzgerald's novel *The Great Gatsby*, for example, we learn toward the end of the story that the highly successful and wealthy Gatsby was originally a man of humble origins. It is only after Gatsby's death that his lower-status father enters the scene. In short, on his route to high status and wealth, the Great Gatsby had severed ties with his lower-status family.

There would be sufficient reason to hypothesize that highly motivated, lower-status Central American immigrant youth might be inclined to achieve in order to become independent of the parental generation as they search for a new identity in the host society. Yet, the very context in which achievement motivation seems to flourish makes the possibility of "traveling up" by breaking family ties untenable, too emotionally costly to be seriously considered.

The majority of my informants stated explicitly, at some point in the research, that their project in the host society was intricately tied to a wish to help others. In a system of reciprocity, they viewed their newly found opportunities in the United States as the chance to reciprocate for all that others had given them. A Salvadorean youth spoke of this when he said:

I now work and study because I want to help my parents. They took me to this country so we could get ahead. It is very hard [to both study and work] because English is not my first language, but I want to help them. And, in the future, I want to be a teacher because I like to help others. I would like to help the Latinos here get ahead in this country. Now I tutor them during the lunch hour. I help them with algebra and biology. I want to be an example to them and to my brothers. I want to help.

The immigrant's plan was far removed from any desire to leave one's folk behind in an upward journey. Such a possibility was found only sporadically in the TAT stories, though occasionally there was some consideration of changing status by giving up relationships.

The following narrative was a response to Card 6BM, in which a short, elderly woman stands with her back turned to a tall, young man. The latter is looking downward with a perplexed expression (for a summary of responses to this card, see Appendix).

Luis was an attorney in the city. He had many offices and was very rich. He lived in a mansion in the northern part of the city, with his children and his spouse. Luis worked well with his co-workers and was a good family man. He was always interested in his children and his spouse. Nobody knew about Luis's past.

His past was a sad past. Ever since he was a little boy he had to work in the streets, shining shoes and selling tickets in buses. But he was interested in studying. That way he achieved his law career.

Once Luis became an attorney he forgot his family. He forgot where he came from. He forgot that he had a mother that struggled for him when he was a little boy.

One day Luis's mother went to visit him in his office. His mother was very sick; she had only a few months to live. When Luis heard this, he became very sad because now he could not do anything for his mother. She had needed medical attention two years before and because he was not next to her then, she was not treated.

Luis could not find the words to beg her to forgive him. But his mother knew that Luis was sorry for what he did. So she forgave him.

When Luis's mother died, he went back to the place where he once lived with her. Being a very rich man, he founded three schools to help the most needy classes in his community.

The manifest content of this story follows an order similar to that of other narratives collected from the young immigrants. Although the story is set in a harmonious, affluent context, soon there is a flashback to a period of deprivation in the hero's childhood. A strong wish to achieve moves Luis from shining shoes in the streets to becoming a high-level attorney in the city. Then the independence from the parental figures—in this case, the mother—surfaces. Leaving his mother behind is unequivocally framed as a serious transgression, for which Luis is severely castigated. This is really the essence of Luis's dark past. Just as "a somebody" by definition translates success into helping others, "a nobody" forgets, turns inward, fails to translate success into the currency of social interdependence and nurturance. The consequences of this callous disregard for his people, for the mother who struggled on his behalf, are devastating: she will die, and there is nothing the rich attorney can do now. It is too late. When she needed medical care, he was too busy being successful to think about his humble people.

As the protagonist gains insight into the consequences of his behavior, he is overwhelmed by feelings of guilt and sadness.

He is paralyzed and can not even bring himself to beg for her forgiveness, yet the all-understanding, sacrificing mother forgives him anyway because she knew he was sorry. It is significant that the story does not end with her death and his sorrow. Her death—literally her sacrifice—brings the hero back to his people, back to the needy classes. Symbolically, building a school is a basic tribute to parental sacrifice. At the end, Luis does learn a hard lesson: one cannot achieve and forget; leaving one's family behind is unacceptable. It is interesting to note that, in the context of American culture, the responses to Card 6BM portray successful executives as leaving home for a career (Henry 1956). The Japanese, in contrast, in the rare stories in which they leave the family to pursue success, are concerned with guilt and with being rejected by an unforgiving mother (De Vos 1973).

The unacceptability of forgetting one's family colored another informant's response to TAT Card 4 (for a summary of responses to this card, see Appendix), in which a "woman is clutching the shoulders of a man whose face and body are averted as if he were trying to pull away from her" (Murray 1943: 19). This is a brief summary of a very long story:

This is a selfish man. He always thought he did not need anyone. One day he lost his job; he lost everything he had. He was broken, and only his family helped him. They found him a new job. He soon started to better himself, and when he was doing well he forgot about all the help his family had given him and he left home.

One day he met a nice girl and fell in love. He was very egoistic and thought only about himself. But she was very nice and honest and didn't leave him. He never again thought about his family and friends until one day when he decided to go visit them. He found his parents' house neglected and empty. He found out that his family had lost everything and had to move to another city. He looked and looked for them but could not find them.

He continued to work hard, and when he had a son he taught him to love his relatives. One day he saw his father by accident. His father had become a beggar. It was not until then that he realized how much harm he had done. He then helped them because he regretted very much what he had done. He then told his own son about his past.

As in other stories, the hero makes it out of a context of deprivation with the aid of his family and then forgets all the help they had given him. The consequences of this behavior are devastating and induce in the hero a severe sense of guilt. Because he regrets his neglect, he not only offers concrete help to his family but also tells his own son all about his past.

Leaving one's family behind is an improbable route for these youths to follow because the very motivational dynamics that drove them to study and work so hard are rooted in a strong sense of obligation and duty to relatives. We have seen how a harsh sense of guilt surfaced among many informants because *they* were sent out of the Central American nightmare when others, parents and siblings, had to remain behind; that *they* now had the opportunity to study in the affluent society when most of their parents had had to leave school to join the labor force at an early age; that *they* may conceivably enter a college or professional training program in the new land, when their siblings' opportunities to do the equivalent in Central America are almost nonexistent.

The TAT stories analyzed here are as much biographical reflections as they are products of the imagination. As a medium for expressing basic interpersonal concerns, however, the TAT also allowed the informants to explore various isomorphic combinations of a fundamental thematic plot. Why was turning to the parents such a recurring theme? Why was turning to the needy family to nurture them so fundamental an interpersonal concern among the new immigrants as to surface almost predictably in their stories? A psychologist unfamiliar with the sociocultural context of achievement motivation might well have hypothesized that their pursuit of achievement was related to a wish for independence from parental or other authority figures; or that the youngsters from economically deprived Central American families were motivated principally by a wish for material self-advancement; or that they were trying to succeed in the host society out of a need to leave their ethnic group behind by becoming modern. In fact, the TAT suggests, as do ethnographic observations and interviews, that a strong wish to achieve correlated closely with a theme of caring for others.

EIGHT

Reality and the Dream in the Inner City: The Legal Ceiling and Other Barriers

HAVING EXPLORED ATTITUDES and interpersonal concerns of the Central American immigrant residents in the inner city, I shall attempt to analyze the consequences for them of contending with the many barriers in educational and other pursuits. Even the most successful of my informants were at times ready to give up on school to join the labor market on a full-time basis. Others, although motivated by the dream, felt overwhelmed by the realities facing them in the inner city: work, solitude, the legal ceiling, and so forth. The school performance of even the brightest and most motivated of them was seriously affected by the cumulative effect of maintaining rigorous work and study schedules. Although the teachers generally favored the new immigrants over their U.S.–born classmates, it would be erroneous to imply that all new arrivals became model students and faced no problems in the inner city schools. Indeed, some serious problems arose.

I must emphasize at the outset that I am not interested in providing a theory of school dropout or failure among the new arrivals. The more challenging question remains why, given their difficult situation, so many of them should succeed in the inner city schools at all. Even though my sample is one of convenience, it is noteworthy that close to 50 percent of my informants were on the honor roll at some time during their high school careers here, and five of them went on to enroll in college, yet even they—Ernesto, Roberto, Angel, Daniel, and Heidi, who at the time of this writing had all embarked on university careers—had reported serious problems in high school and considered, at one point or another, leaving school to work full-time. Others could no longer tolerate the pressures resulting from work and study and chose simply to work full-time.

One of the major problems facing the new arrivals was "gate-keeping," techniques employed in the schools, notably in the counseling office, which seemed to me to prevent new arrivals from enrolling in a pedagogically sound program of study (see Erickson and Shultz 1981; Cicourel and Kitsuse 1963). The effect of this failure was all too often a sense of academic helplessness among the new arrivals.

Gatekeeping

The new arrivals entered the U.S. educational system at an Intake Center, in a decayed inner-city building, where they were tested on oral English proficiency. They were also given written tests on the basic structure of English and mathematics. Based on the results of these tests and on the official school records from the country of origin, each new arrival was placed at a theoretically appropriate grade level. Those immigrants without copies of their transcripts had to prepare a formal affidavit indicating the courses they had taken in Central America, the grades, and the number of credits received. In the "intake" procedure there were major flaws, some of which would be hilarious were it not for the fact that the future of youngsters was in part being decided. A vignette will make the point. During the early part of my research I spent a week talking to personnel at the center and otherwise observing the process by which the new arrivals were enrolled in the American educational system. Other tasks took me back to the center an additional number of times. As I observed the way the new arrivals were tested, I was shocked to find out that the person responsible for administering the tests did not speak English fluently! In fact, her accent was so heavy that I had difficulty understanding her as she read the instructions to the tests. How the recent arrivals, with their limited English skills, were supposed to understand and follow any instructions is beyond my comprehension. The rationale seemed to be that ethnic individuals would somehow make the new arrival's initiation into the American schooling system less threatening.

Upon completing this *rite de passage*, each of the new immigrants was assigned to a particular school at a specified grade level. Upon arrival at the school and theoretically in coordination with the recommendations given at the Intake Center, a counselor and the student would agree on a program of study. At Joaquin High School there was only one bilingual counselor for about 350 Spanish-speaking immigrant students— among them the new arrivals from Central America, in addition to Mexican students and South Americans mostly from Ecuador, Peru, and Colombia. This counselor had been a teacher who, as she put it, "had had it in the classroom" and maneuvered her way, with the approval of the school administration, to become a temporary counselor.* She had been on this temporary assignment for over three years. At Jefferson High there was no bilingual counselor, but only a coordinator of bilingual education.

The ratio of 350 students to one counselor is hardly ideal, particularly in view of the special needs of this student population. The new arrivals, having experienced the horrors of war, and now living away from their nuclear families and having to work while attending school, faced unique burdens that would conceivably make their demands on the bilingual counselor all the more acute. The counselor, however, saw her primary duty, not as addressing any such concerns, but rather as processing the new arrivals mechanically and with as little personal contact as possible, into a nonacademic program of study. "They are not college material," she told me more than once. This basic premise prevailed beyond the four walls of the counseling office. In fact, I did not fully comprehend the comments of counselors, teachers, and other school officials, at an early stage in the research, who kept telling me, "We are not an academic school," or "This inner-city school does not emphasize college preparation." Eventually I discovered that there was only one academic high school in that school district. The basic assumption was that the inner-city students, including the recent arrivals, would not go on to enroll in college. Therefore the school staff in gen-

---

* The counselor's first language was Spanish. She spoke English well, but with a heavy accent.

eral, and the counselor in particular, were essentially uncon-
cerned with matters of college preparation.

Joaquin's bilingual counselor, herself a Central American,
seemed remote from her work and unable to empathize with the
new arrivals of lower status. She complained that she could not
perform effectively, given the large number of students assigned
to her. Thus, rather than designing productive individual plans
of study for each student, she resorted to the application of
wholesale formulae that often proved incompatible with the students' educational needs. Her working assumption was that the
lower-status recent arrivals could not possibly be college material. Therefore, her objective was not to prepare them for a potential college career but rather to enroll them in a program that
would simply graduate them from high school and perhaps aid
them in entering a professional training program. Yet the program of study required for college entrance goes beyond the
basic requirements for graduation from high school. The nonacademic programs that would allow the recent arrivals to graduate fell far short of qualifying them to enter college.

Many of my informants reported being extremely unhappy
about the courses to which they were assigned. A chronic com-
plaint was that the counseling office assigned them to courses
far below their capabilities. In both the mathematics and the English programs, they were usually enrolled in overcrowded,
low-level courses. In math, in particular, the courses at both
sites were entry level, even though in Central America informants had taken and passed algebra, and sometimes even
geometry.

Marcos, a senior from El Salvador, had taken both algebra and
geometry at home; he had been a good student and had received
high marks in both subjects. When he began school in the United
States, the counseling office had enrolled him in introductory algebra, and he was unable to convince the counselor that he had
in fact studied beyond algebra and that it would be a waste of
time to go back to an introductory course. As he related his case
to me, he even made a joke *No soy un cangrejo, no quiero ir para
atras!* ("I am not a crab, I don't want to go backward!").* Some

---

* This metaphor refers to Spanish-language usage in which crabs are said to
walk backward. Thus, saying "I am not a crab, I don't want to go backward"
means "I want to go forward (better myself) and not backward."

informants came to believe that the education they encountered in the inner city was indeed inferior to their prior schooling in Central America (see also Vlach 1984.) Marcos noted that part of the problem was that his Salvadorean school record did not specify the courses he had taken; it stated only that he had taken Math 1, Math 2, and Math 3, which were credited at the Intake Center only as arithmetic, and he was enrolled in beginning algebra.

Like many other informants, Marcos felt helpless about wasting his time. Yet he maintained a pragmatic attitude: "My objective now is to graduate, even if I fall asleep in class." Some of my informants in similar situations were eventually able to manipulate the system and to enroll in more advanced, and challenging, courses. They were among my most successful informants, those who went on to enter the university.

Another gatekeeping strategy was to mystify the process of applying to college. Rather than encouraging and aiding those seeking information, the counselor would systematically put roadblocks in the youngsters' path, giving them hopelessly complex entrance and financial aid applications, in English, without any advice or guidance. The "gate-opening" approach adopted by some successful immigrants was to organize visits themselves to local colleges and universities in order to gain information at first hand.

Perhaps the most damaging gatekeeping was done in the name of the noble idea of teaching English as a second language. The ESL program was, according to teachers at both sites, the school's own inner ghetto. The classes were overcrowded and understaffed, with enrollments of 30 to 35 students.* Though the target number for entry-level ESL classes was 25 students, the teachers regularly had to operate with more students than they could possibly properly teach. Two teachers also complained that their bilingual aides were unreliable and incapable. One aide, for example, was absent on a regular basis while she was suing the school district over an injury sustained on the job. Because the case was being litigated, the district refused to assign a new aide to the classroom. The teachers themselves felt quite helpless about their situation but tried to do the best they

---

* I counted 37 foreign students in one entry-level ESL class.

could. One teacher confided that at least four of her immigrant Central American students should have been moved into the regular English program, which would not, however, accept any transfers from ESL because it too was operating at maximum capacity.

The inner-city teachers had many other problems to report, among others—almost universally—the lack of proper and up-to-date teaching materials. The ESL and bilingual teachers in particular felt that they had more work than the regular teaching staff (non-bilingual/non-ESL) but less status vis-à-vis other teachers and school administrators. As one teacher put it, "They think we can't teach anything else, and that is why we go into bilingual." These factors contributed to a feeling of alienation among the teachers. A common strategy for dealing with their own sense of helplessness was to routinize all classroom activities to an absurd point, where teaching often seemed secondary to pedagogically irrelevant tasks. In one classroom, the new arrivals spent an entire week watching movies on the civil-rights movement. A good idea, except that the southern accents that predominated in the movies were incomprehensible to the recent arrivals, who just fell asleep in the classroom.

The students' responses to the difficult situation were varied. Some would try to recruit the help and power of a sympathetic individual within the administration to rectify a problem, such as inappropriate course assignments. Student self-help groups also emerged, to help with homework and particularly to find out about post-high-school opportunities. A number of my senior informants volunteered during their lunch hour to help the younger recent arrivals with their homework and other issues. Other students seemed to take a pragmatic attitude probably related to their vulnerable legal status in the host society: they chose "not to make waves," to endure the boredom, pass the courses, and eventually graduate. Still others, especially ninth- and tenth-graders, were overcome by a terrible sense of boredom and a feeling of the futility of the school routine. Apparently less driven by a sense of responsibility, they began to turn to one another for support and diversion. They would cut classes more often than their older peers, and their school records would eventually reflect this pattern. The older students at the more advanced grade-levels would have survived this phase and would tend to be more judicious and less likely to cut classes or drop out of school, being that much closer to graduation. The relative immaturity of the younger new arrivals may well account for their lack of the strong sense of responsibility that drove the older students to do well in school. Or, conversely, it was among the older students that the sense of duty and responsibility toward parents surfaced most forcefully. This characteristic was captured in the projective TAT data on the older males (17 to 19-year-olds), who most often constructed stories in which the protagonist works hard in school to achieve and turns to help the parental characters (see Table 7.1). Admittedly, though, this sample is too small to permit any wide generalizations in this regard. The fact that many of the recently arrived ninth- and tenth-graders who left Central America within the past five years were in the 9 to 14-year-old age bracket at the time of their departure is also important. While in Central America, they, being younger, would have been less likely to be terrorized by the prospect of being drafted by the military or taken away by the guerrillas. Likewise, none of the youngsters in this group reported having had a peer disappear, as had the older informants. These youngsters simply lacked the perspective shared by the older informants: that comparatively they were much better off in the host society, and that it was now their duty to take full advantage of their new opportunities.

Some of these youngsters may also have been affected by the so-called "vulnerable age phenomenon" observed among children who migrate between the ages of 6 and 11 (see Inbar 1976). Research in Israel and the United States seems to suggest that those children tend to do less well academically than either younger or older children undergoing the same changes. My major reservation with respect to applying the vulnerable age phenomenon paradigm to the Central American data is that the crises endured by most of the new arrivals go far beyond migration at any age. Their personal experience of the war in Central America would undoubtedly interact with other variables such as age and sex to affect learning in the classrooms.

Arroyo and Eth have argued that many immigrant children traumatized in the Central American war zone may suffer post-traumatic stress disorder. They present psychiatric case descriptions of a 5-year-old boy and a 17-year-old girl, both brutally victimized in Central America, both beset by serious problems in schools. After examining these and other traumatized children, the authors conclude:

These Central American refugee youngsters have been targets of various assaults, with each assault varying in its developmental point of entry, its intensity, its duration and its psychopathological result. Unfortunately, the chronically malnourished and deprived young child is compromised early. As with the child who is immunologically suppressed and vulnerable to virulent infectious agents, the war-ravaged child who has experienced traumatic stress is gravely predisposed to further opportunistic insults in the form of separations, a forced uprooting, a tumultuous resettlement. However, having identified their special circumstances, the war-traumatized child's prognosis becomes more favorable with further study and timely interventions. As a growing segment of our society, it is essential that some preparation be made to adequately meet the needs of this special population. [Arroyo and Eth 1986: 103–20]

During my year of fieldwork in the inner city, I never heard a teacher or counselor refer a youngster to a psychological or medical clinic. In fact, many teachers in the inner city seemed utterly unaware of, and uninterested in, the situation from which the new arrivals had escaped. To my query whether she thought the situation in Central America could potentially affect her students' social adaptation, the bilingual counselor responded, "That is not my concern; my concern is with what happens within the walls of this school."

Work and Schooling

Ernesto began working full-time during his senior year of high school. While in the tenth and eleventh grades, he managed to survive, working only part-time, four or five hours a day, mostly in restaurants and as a gardener. His living arrangement was precarious: he moved from place to place, a total of six times, living mostly with Salvadorean families who would give him a place to sleep, sometimes without requesting him to pay a share of the rent. As he began his senior year, a series of quarrels made it impossible for Ernesto to remain living with the family he had been with for months. At that point he "moved" into his old car and lived there for about three weeks. He would eat, bathe, and wash his clothes at his friends' apartments. A sympathetic teacher eventually found out about this arrangement and invited Ernesto to sleep at his house, until he could find a more permanent residence. At that point Ernesto felt it was necessary to find full-time work. The manager of the restaurant where he had been working agreed to take him on, full-time, and his new schedule as a "salad boy" was from 4 P.M., right after school, until after midnight. The increase in salary allowed him to pay his share of the rent for a minuscule apartment with three other Salvadoreans.

Ernesto had always been an honor roll student, but the heavy new schedule eventually took its toll. In the eleventh grade, while he worked only part-time, Ernesto had missed a total of 19 classes. Yet in the twelfth grade, when he worked full-time, he missed a total of 78 classes! His grade point average (GPA), which had been an impeccable 4.0 during his junior year, fell to 2.9 for the senior year, or just below a B average. Ernesto himself was keenly aware of this downward pattern, which he knew was directly related to his brutal work schedule:

This is because . . . I had to work full-time . . . 40 hours per week during my senior year. I worked until after midnight every day. I would go into work at 4 P.M. and I would be back here [his apartment] at 1 or 2 in the morning. . . . I did not feel like studying. Sometimes, before exams, I did push myself to study until 3 or 4 in the morning. Then I had to get up at 7 A.M. to go to school. And I did not get out of school until 3:30 P.M. I would then take the bus to work . . . and back here to sleep a little. . . . Many times I fell asleep and missed classes!

I was supposed to start working at 3:30 P.M., so I had a talk with the manager. I said, "Look, I can't get here before 4 P.M. because I go to school until 3:30." He said it was OK, as long as I was at work before 4:30. And I left work after midnight. When I got home I felt very tired, I could not concentrate on my homework. My entire body hurt and my brain was tired. . . . I had headaches, tremendous headaches from all the work. My eyes would burn when I tried to do homework at night. I would just fall asleep. The next day I would get up at 7 A.M. to get ready to go to school. Sometimes I just could not keep up with this routine. . . . Mr. Bozza used to tell me, "Ernesto you are always falling asleep in class, you cannot continue doing this." I would say, "I really cannot stay awake. I put everything I have into school, but I cannot keep up with this," but I somehow continued and I graduated. I wanted to study, I put all my efforts into studying. But it was really hard. My grades were not the same [as before].

As already noted, 68 percent of the new arrivals in my sample worked while attending school full-time (see Table 5.1). What effect did the work patterns have on the schooling of the new arrivals? Only three of my informants, all males, worked full-time while attending school full-time, and all three reported that their schooling was seriously affected. Each of them had considered at some point leaving school and dedicating himself to work. Two of them had worked in restaurants, and one in a market. The two seniors went on to graduate, and the junior went on to the twelfth grade.

Those working part-time had heavy work schedules, which sometimes interfered with their school obligations. Their part-time jobs were concentrated in the service professions—among the young men, busboy (restaurant), dishwasher (restaurant), and janitor; and among the young women, maid, baby-sitter, and elderly care. Most of them worked between 15 and 30 hours per week and shared at least part of their salaries with relatives either in the United States or back in Central America.

Laura, a 15-year-old from El Salvador, spent every Tuesday, Thursday, and Friday afternoon, and all of Saturday, helping her mother clean houses. Estela, a 16-year-old from El Salvador, worked with an aunt at a local fast-food restaurant from 4 P.M. until 8 P.M. every day after school. Both were honor-roll students, yet both reported having not as much time for studying as they felt necessary. Their work was physically demanding, and at the end of the day they just had no energy to face homework or to prepare properly for a test.

The Legal Ceiling: "What Will I Do After Completing High School?"

Silvia found out during her second semester in an American high school that she would not be able to enroll in college. She was a junior and had earned a straight 4.0 GPA during her first semester of high school in the United States. All of her teachers agreed that she had been a model student: she was polite and, above all, terribly motivated to learn English. Toward the end of her second semester, something happened. Silvia's teachers noted that she began cutting classes and that she would turn in sloppy homework; her grades had slipped markedly. Her classroom manner changed too. She seemed less attentive. One of her teachers thought that Silvia was depressed.

Like many other new immigrants, Silvia had been sent out of her native El Salvador, in the midst of the escalating terror. At one point, she said, the war had made it literally impossible for them to even go into the streets. At the age of 16, she and a younger brother were sent by her parents to live with an aunt in the safety of the United States. Her aunt worked in a candy factory. She and her husband had been in the United States for over 15 years. They had no children of their own, and they did not expect or want Silvia or her brother to work. One morning Silvia's aunt came to see me in desperation: Silvia had given up on school. She was no longer interested in her studies.

Silvia herself seemed depressed.* At first she almost refused to talk to me. My initial attempts at establishing some communication were sabotaged by the monosyllabic responses that only a depressed teenager can produce. Only after her aunt insisted that I was there to help them did Silvia begin slowly to open up. She seemed undisturbed about my chats with her aunt and her teachers, yet her studied nonchalance betrayed a repressed anger under a surface attitude of "well, I just don't care about school, all I want now is to get a job." In retrospect Silvia noted that, as she settled down in the United States, she had decided to pursue the profession she had dreamed about since she was a little girl: she would become a nurse. Her plan, like that of other young immigrants, was to return one day with her American-acquired skills to set herself up in an important position in her native land, where her parents and other relatives remained. Eventually she told me what had been bothering her: a few weeks into her second semester as a junior she discovered that, without residency status, she would have to pay extraordinarily high fees even if she were accepted into nursing school. "Where can I get that much money?" she asked me.

* Those ignorant of the personal lives of the youngsters commonly interpreted such depression as evidence of "Latin flat-affect," as one teacher put it, or even "laziness."

Like most of the new arrivals I encountered during the course of my research, Silvia was facing what I call a "legal ceiling." The complex legal technicalities regarding the rights and privileges of undocumented aliens residing in the United States are a source of confusion to the new students. Although universities and colleges throughout the country generally require them to possess some kind of formal status such as citizenship, legal permanent residence, student visa, or political asylum status, a California court ruled in 1985 that it was illegal for colleges and universities to bar undocumented residents from enrolling in their institutions. In the view of my informants, it appears that very few of the new arrivals were fully aware of their rights and options in the light of this decision. Most *ilegales* who intended to go on to college were shocked and depressed when they found out that colleges and universities required them to be legal to enroll. As an 18-year-old from Nicaragua put it, right after graduating from high school:

My problem now is that I am illegal. If I was a citizen, I would now be in college. . . . I did not even apply to college. Why would I want to apply? What would I put down where they ask for my "Residency Status"? Now they say it is illegal to keep undocumented students out of the university. This is new, so now I have to wait until the next deadline to apply. The greatest prejudice against me is not having the residency here. The reason why I do not have a better job is that I do not have the residency. If I had the residency, I would have many possibilities to find better jobs. Also, I would be able to bring my family here.

Herman commented more generally on the experiences that many recent arrivals perceived as resulting from their lack of documentation:

Without the residency life is very hard. Students here lose hope [*se desmoralizan*]. In my own case, when I realized that I needed the residency to be able to go to college, I did not want to study any more, I did not want to go to school. I thought that it was impossible to study a career here without having my [residency] papers. So all I wanted to do . . . was to get a good job to send money to El Salvador. My objective was to help my family. Their economic situation is bad, my father's salary is not enough for them to live on.

During my senior year I felt very depressed. I kept asking myself "Why continue this? Why work and go to school if you won't get into the university without having papers?" I felt very low. The first thing they ask in the [college] application form is . . . "Are you a citizen, a resident, a refugee?" That made me feel depressed. And the other [Central American] students, most of them are illegal. They feel the same way. They say, "Why keep studying, I'm a wetback [*soy un mojado*] and the first thing they ask you in the college application is for your Green Card Number?" Most of them are "wetbacks." . . . They would say in class, "How do you expect me to keep studying hard if I have no Green Card? What will I do after completing high school?"

John Ogbu (1974 and 1978) has explored the complex relationships between access to the opportunity structure and the schooling strategies of minority students. The Central American case allows us to isolate certain specific adaptations to this critical variable, the legal requirements for entrance into college. As this wave of recent arrivals becomes increasingly aware of the legal ceiling that they may face, those without documentation that will enable them to enroll in college begin to develop strategies to deal with the barrier. I became fully aware of the importance of the legal ceiling toward the end of the study. There seemed to be three strategies for dealing with the legal ceiling, and undoubtedly others will emerge as the new arrivals become more fully aware of their rights under the law. Some of those informants who had earlier expressed a wish to enter college seemed to shift toward applying for a professional training program, such as in computers, dental assistance, cosmetology, diesel mechanics, and the like—programs that did not require proof of residency. Others, like Silvia, seemed to become depressed and anxious to enter the labor market at once. Working to make money became a priority among those who felt the legal ceiling would prevent them from even applying to college. Some informants chose to maneuver around the system to fulfill their dream of achieving *universitario* status. Three of them pursued their cases to the point of involving high-ranking administrators in the universities they wished to attend and were eventually able to enroll in college.

We have considered the obstacles to achievement that the new arrivals encounter most frequently within their educational experiences, and how they deal with those obstacles: gatekeeping; employment outside of school hours; legal residency. Common to them all, in addition, is the legacy of war and economic scarcity in Central America, which appears to have been totally overlooked by school officials. Two additional issues have also created certain problems for the new arrivals. One relates to the fact that some immigrants had been removed from school in Central America as a direct consequence of the war. The parents of one informant felt that it was too risky to keep him in school: several students had disappeared, and both the army and the guerrillas had conducted aggressive recruiting campaigns in the site, so he stayed out of school and went to work the land with his father for a number of years. Upon entering school in the United States he was in an awkward position: at age 17 he felt very much a man, but his teachers treated him essentially like a boy. For some of the younger, less self-regulated students, a problem emerged relative to the living arrangements in the inner city. Lack of proper supervision at home because of the working schedules of the adults in charge seemed to affect the schooling of some new arrivals, a number of whom went home to an empty house. As a consequence, some of them had no one to turn to for help with schoolwork, even when the tasks were in Spanish. For some informants, who routinely stayed after classes to do homework in school, the problem was simply lack of space to concentrate and do their work.

NINE

Hermes in the Barrios:
A Psychocultural Critique
of Motivation Theory

HAVING CONSIDERED in some detail the anatomy of the new immigrant's wish to achieve in the context of resettling in the United States, I have argued that the dream to become somebody through hard work and study flourished in a specific cluster of social perceptions and interpersonal concerns. On the instrumental level the evidence seems to support the argument for an ultimate goal, namely to help others, such as relatives still in Central America, in a material way. Among many new immigrants the wish to study seems to be related to a subtle expressive need to justify parental sacrifices by achieving what the parents could not. The youngsters' underlying feelings of guilt at having been able to leave Central America, or even at having one or both parents struggling in the United States, also fueled their desire to succeed.

In this specific context "becoming somebody" was not associated with a wish to gain independence from family and friends. Very much to the contrary: "becoming somebody" was viewed as the way to fulfill the dream of helping those who had sacrificed on one's behalf. In fact, as noted in Chapter 7, leaving relatives behind in the context of achieving success was an avenue the new immigrants did not pursue. Routinely, my informants framed their efforts in the new land as a way to reciprocate, to pay back their parents.

In this concluding chapter, I shall explore the specific motivational pattern I have identified among the new arrivals in the context of the larger theoretical work on achievement motivation by David McClelland and his associates. My thesis is that their achievement-independence cluster, useful as it may be to explore a culture-bound motivational pattern adapted to certain social and interpersonal atmospheres, is largely inadequate to explain the motivational dynamics manifest in new immigrant Hispanics.

Other People, Other Places, Other Times: The Dangers of Theoretical Overextension

It has long been argued that, almost since their inception as separate disciplines, anthropology and psychology have approached certain basic questions regarding human functioning from remarkably different perspectives (see Spiro 1954: 19–30). This is perhaps most evident in the way the two disciplines have gone about exploring the wider implications of their findings. Psychologists, for example, have often argued for the universalistic applications of their findings, be they derived from upper-middle-class Viennese hysterics, American college undergraduates, or even laboratory rats. Research on rats has, in fact, produced some adventurous cross-species generalizations that are based on a shaky and "audacious assumption of species equivalence" (Murray 1951: 435). Anthropologists, on the other hand, have traditionally sinned in the other direction. Once they agreed that culture is the nature of humans (Geertz 1973: 3–83) and that societies reflect the infinite plasticity of the human spirit, they engaged in more or less systematic "negative-instancing" to Western-based models with universalistic pretensions. Thus, although Freud believed in the pan-human applicability of his model of human functioning, it was Bronislaw Malinowski, the father of modern anthropology, who took issue with the universality of its cornerstone, the Oedipus complex (1927, 1929). Malinowski argued that there was no evidence to support the existence of the Oedipus complex as described by Freud among the matrilineal Trobriand Islanders; rather, he said, the Trobrianders developed their own "matrilineal complex."[*]

* For a thorough consideration of the ensuing Freudian-Malinowski debate, see Spiro's judicious 1982 book; see also Jones 1925.

When American and European psychologists concluded that the period of adolescent turbulence was rooted in certain biological maturational processes that were similarly pan-human, it took the mother of modern anthropology, Margaret Mead, to question its cross-cultural validity (1928). In her famous (more recently infamous) book, *Coming of Age in Samoa* (1928), Mead argued that among Samoan girls no such period of adolescent turbulence was evident: the passage from childhood to womanhood in Samoan culture was not traumatic, as it was in the West. Therefore, Mead concluded, rather than assume some pan-human universal process at work, we must turn our attention to specific sociocultural patterns and their consequences in the human psyche.*

More recently, Nancy Scheper-Hughes (1985: 291–317) has investigated the inadequacy of universalistic models suggesting an innate basis for the process of mother-child "bonding." She has argued that

Theories of innate maternal scripts such as "bonding," "maternal thinking," or "maternal instincts" are both culture and history bound, the reflection of a very specific and very recent reproductive strategy: to give birth to a few babies and to invest heavily in each one. This is a reproductive strategy that was a stranger to most European history through the early modern period, and it does not reflect the "maternal thinking" of a great many women living in the Third World today where an alternative strategy holds: to give birth to many children, invest selectively based on culturally derived favored characteristics, and hope that a few would survive infancy and the early years of life. [1985: 310]

By alluding to these ongoing disputes, I wish to illustrate that there is a history of tension between psychological and anthropological research as it relates to the application of certain findings to other people, in other places, in other times. In particular, I would like to explore further the implications of my findings among recent arrivals from Central America to the study of achievement motivation as it has been traditionally framed in the scholarly literature. In fact, with a few exceptions (see De Vos 1973), there has been a general lack of concern in academic psychology with systematically capturing the sociocultural per-

* For a critique of Mead's Samoan study, see Freeman 1983.

mutations in achievement motivation among different cultural and ethnic groups.

Achievement Need and Independence Need: A Universal Complex or an Anglo-American Oicotype?

David C. McClelland and his associates pioneered the systematic study of human motivation; any serious consideration of achievement motivation must consider their contributions (see, e.g., McClelland 1955, 1961, 1984; McClelland et al. 1953, 1958; Stewart 1982; Spence 1983). Influenced by some basic Freudian principles, McClelland and his colleagues view human motivations as related to affective processes that can be explored by turning to the products of fantasy. They concentrated their efforts on capturing achievement motivation, which they define as the need for "competition with a standard of excellence" (McClelland et al. 1953: 161), in the products of human fantasy. By the use of projective tests, including the TAT, and also through the study of folklore, more specifically folktales, they attempted to document achievement themes under various experimental conditions (McClelland et al. 1953: 97–161). And they searched in certain cultural and family dynamics for the origins of achievement motivation:

In the case of achievement motivation, the situation should involve a "standard of excellence," presumably imposed on the child by the culture, or more particularly by the parents as representatives of the culture, and the behavior should involve either "competition" with those standards of excellence or attempts to meet them which, if successful, provide positive affect or, if unsuccessful, negative affect. It follows that those cultures or families which stress "competition with standards of excellence" or which insist *that the child be able to perform certain tasks well by himself*—such cultures or families should produce children with high achievement motivation (McClelland et al. 1953: 275).

The key points are (1) that the wish to compete with and for excellence is taught; (2) that it is presumably taught more, or better, by certain cultural or familial groups than others; and (3) that successfully meeting the standards of excellence is, in and of itself, a source of positive affect.

Precisely how, then, and in what social contexts, is motivation taught? What are the specific processes significant in the training of achievement motivation? How do cultures teach children to achieve? McClelland's hypothesis is that "individuals with high achievement motivation will have been forced to master problems on their own more often and earlier than individuals with low achievement motivation" (McClelland et al. 1953: 276). Subjects with high achievement motivation were apparently forced by their caretakers to master environmental tasks on their own more often, and earlier, than people with lower achievement motivation. Thus, in this model achievement motivation and independence training are intimately related.* McClelland's group identified a number of specific variables that foster achievement motivation. Upon close scrutiny, these variables give us a glimpse of the general sociocultural ethos that permeates his model.

McClelland has written that within the family a certain degree of perceived parental aloofness and even a certain felt lack of love are associated with high achievement motivation. For example, among American college students, "a 'felt lack of love' is associated with high n Achievement. The largest single correlation involves the rejection attributed to the fathers by their sons; that is, sons who felt their fathers had rejected them had higher n Achievement scores than those who felt their fathers had loved them and accepted them. . . . Sons with high n Achievement tend to perceive their fathers as unfriendly and unhelpful." In fact, in a sample of American college students, those who "give evidence of being very 'close' to their parents in their admiration of them and perception of them as particularly loving and helpful do not for the most part score high on n Achievement. On the contrary, it is the students who see their parents as 'distant'—unfriendly, severe, unsuccessful—who have high n Achievement scores" (McClelland et al. 1953: 279–81). The key words here are "unfriendly, severe, unsuccessful"—the perceptions that presumably fostered achievement motivation among American college students. In brief, according to this model,

---

* For a detailed consideration of the relationship between achievement and independence training, see also Rosen and D'Andrade 1965. For a recent statement on achievement motivation, also influenced by McClelland's works, see Spence 1983.

achievement motivation typically emerges in a climate of paternal aloofness, even rejection.

Subsequent studies among American high-school students led McClelland and his followers to conclude that there are optimal levels of perceived parental aloofness that are associated with high achievement motivation: either too much or too little perceived rejection may be counterproductive to the emergence of a robust achievement motive (see also Rosen and D'Andrade 1965: 375–99).

In McClelland's model, then, achievement motivation is intimately related to a socialization pattern that puts emphasis on the training of independence, through unfriendly and severe parental practices. The more and the earlier parents pushed their children to become independent and to turn to themselves to solve problems, the more the motivation to achieve would be fostered. High achievement-motive mothers teach their would-be high achievement-motive children that they are independent, and they must know that they are on their own to solve problems. In fact, Veroff found that mothers with high achievement-motive were somewhat distant and saw their "children as interfering with their use of time" (in Stewart 1982: 114). Indeed, the retrospective perceptions of high-achieving American college undergraduates give the general impression of a familiar ethos that encouraged early independence in an almost stereotypical Anglo-Saxon polar climate.

McClelland's model captures an unmistakably Protestant socialization pattern rooted in a specific ethic, embedded within a socioeconomic climate. Indeed, one of his objectives (see LeVine 1967) was to explore how "the Protestant ethic" (Weber 1958) was translated into concrete socialization patterns adapted to a capitalistic mode of production. According to this model, increasing industrial, technological, and bureaucratic specialization would require workers to discharge their duties independently and autonomously. In this case, they argue, socialization for achievement occurs in an atmosphere of severity and coldness, which breeds self-reliance, individualism, and the sense that one stands on his own at an early age. McClelland and associates were not content, however, with identifying and documenting the dynamics of what is in my estimation an Anglo-

American and Northern European oicotype, or variant adapted
to a specific cultural climate. Like some other psychologists,
McClelland claimed that his model had a wider, indeed a universal, application to "children in all cultures" (McClelland et al.
1953: 289). Here, I think, is where his explanatory system becomes increasingly problematic.

De Vos has specifically cautioned that McClelland's model
may not "fit well" the evidence from the cross-cultural record.
Years of research among Japanese and Japanese-Americans have
led him to conclude that

The psychological theory of achievement motivation presented by
McClelland and others . . . does not fit Japan well in all its contentions.
In the samples of TAT materials obtained in Chicago and in various settings in rural and urban Japan we have found a pervasive preoccupation with achievement and accomplishment, no matter what group of
Japanese was tested, but the achievement imagery differs from that
found in American samples in respect to the context within which it
appears. Throughout, the Japanese materials also show both very high
need affiliation and concern with nurturance and dependence, conflict-
ing with the American data, which usually suggest a negative correspondence between the appearance of need achievement and need affiliation. [De Vos 1973: 180]

Before examining how the Central American data raise doubts
about McClelland's proposition that achievement motivation is
intimately related to a form of rugged individualism, I shall consider how McClelland went about exploring the universalistic
applications of his model. After all, he wrote, "We do not want
to develop a theory of motivation or a method of scoring for
achievement motivation which will apply only to middle-class
White American males. The theory as stated is more general
than that and *should apply to children in all cultures*" (McClelland
et al. 1953: 289, my emphasis). To test whether the achieve-
ment/individualism model was valid to children in all cultures,
McClelland and his associates turned to a thematic analysis of
achievement content of folktales among eight North American
Indian groups. They then related the thematic content of the
tales among the different Indian groups to each group's independence training (McClelland et al. 1953: 289–97). McClelland's
message is that those eight North American Indian groups some-

how represent the remaining children in all cultures, which is really incomprehensible to most modern anthropologists, as is also their treatment of some other ethnographic materials.

First, instead of collecting and analyzing multiple versions of the tales, as most folklorists would have advised them to do, they seemed to rely on composite versions of the tales. A characteristic of folklore is the multiple existence of any given folkloristic text (see Dundes 1965: 1–3; Bascom 1965: 25–33). In fact, their method of presenting the folklore data makes it impossible to confirm the validity of their thematic interpretations independently. Second, it is not at all clear that they were able to identify folkloristic oicotypes for specific Indian tribes. Indeed, the argument would have been stronger had they been able to identify that folktale *A*, for example, a Navaho oicotype, is related to a specific cultural independence-training pattern *and* is not to be found among other tribes that do not share that independence-training pattern. As they present their case, the possibility is not ruled out that high-achievement-content tale *A* from high independence-training tribe *A* is not present in low independence-training tribe *B*.

A third, and certainly an important, problem with McClelland's anthropological modus operandi is that rather than relying on their own ethnographic field work to rate independence training among the various North American tribes, they used as their source the ethnographically suspect Human Relations Area Files (HRAF), which have been severely criticized on grounds of accuracy and reliability (see Barnouw 1979: 145–52).

In short, then, their own highly problematic test of the achievement-individualism cluster among the Indian groups makes it clear that the cross-cultural test of the model is far from satisfactory, yet throughout his latter writings McClelland continued to claim a cross-cultural basis for the model. In his classic *The Achieving Society* (1961), he again turned to folklore, this time to capture the very essence of achievement motivation in the mythological figure of Hermes:

Basically the story deals with how he [Hermes] steals the cattle of his older brother Apollo on the day he is born. He clearly has high *n* Achievement: "It did not take long to prove his prowess to the immortal gods. Born in the morning, in the noonday he performed upon a lyre, in the evening he stole the cattle of the archer-god Apollo." The achievement imagery is of two general types. Great stress is laid on how cunning a schemer Hermes is to outwit his powerful older brother, even though he is only a baby. "He is litigious, skillful at making the worse appear the better reason. He lies brazenly to Apollo. He tries a mixture of trickery, bluffing, flattery, and cajoling to persuade Apollo to let him keep his cattle, and it succeeds." [McClelland 1961: 302]

According to McClelland, Hermes shares the essential traits of the "trickster hero." He is "an outrageous liar and a thief. He swears, after stealing his brother's cattle, both to Apollo and Zeus that he is as innocent as the newborn babe he is and that he has not seen the cattle." Finally, Hermes does derive great pleasure "out of his schemes" (McClelland 1961: 302–3).

Whether Hermes is the achievement-motive archetype or a psychopathic archetype is surely debatable. What remains curious, and revealing, is that McClelland should find in the figure of Hermes the essence of achievement for the reason that he is driven by a strong desire for independence from his family and for material self-advancement, evidently at the family's expense. In fact, Hermes's earliest acts include stealing cattle from his own brother and lying to his father for the sake of self-advancement. The interpersonal family atmosphere in which, according to McClelland, the achievement archetype emerges ("trickery, bluffing, flattery, and cajoling") is quite remarkable!

According to this model, achievement motivation flourishes within a rather specific family dynamic, that is, within a matrix that trains youngsters to become independent of others. Indeed, high n Achievement subjects perceived their parents as somewhat aloof and distant. They were taught, and seemed to learn, that they are on their own in this world and must face the environment by themselves as early as possible. Indeed, rather than orienting the self toward the family in order to achieve, they seem to have to turn away from the family. According to McClelland the symbolism in Hermes's story dramatically captures a family climate in which n Achievement grows. Little Hermes not only learns to achieve by not becoming paralyzed by family obligations, but in fact he early and violently turns away from his immediate family.

Familistic Charity and the Dream

McClelland's analysis of achievement motivation would suggest that the most successful of the recent Central American immigrants should be self-reliant individualists, "traveling with light affective baggage," wishing to leave their parents and other folk behind in their upward journey. Accordingly, these youngsters should be struggling for independence from their parents, perhaps to gain materialistic self-advancement to compensate for being from economically unsuccessful family backgrounds. The theory may correctly address motivational issues among middle-class White Protestants, but it does not fit well the subtle motivational dynamics encountered among the new immigrants from war-torn Central America. Since this model, based largely upon salient aspects of a Protestant ethic, does not adequately explain their motivational concerns, how then does their own religious life affect the new arrivals?

The religious experience of the new arrivals has indeed influenced their adaptation to the new land. Most of those in my sample are either Catholic or Evangelical (Pentecostal, particularly the Guatemalans and Salvadoreans).* From a Weberian standpoint (Weber 1958), the church seems to offer the new arrivals a "web of meanings" (Geertz 1973) in the process of upheaval and change. Almost universally, my informants reported attending Spanish-speaking services and other church-related activities where the majority of the congregation was Hispanic, largely of Central American origin. Familiar religious symbols and ritual lend some sense of continuity in belonging with other Central Americans in the barrios. In addition to lending some order and meaning to the process of change, issues relating to status and the experience of power among the low-status new arrivals are also important. Religious communion, as a collective representation, consists of participation and literal ingestion of sacred power (De Vos and Suarez-Orozco 1987). The powerless gain power, albeit temporarily, in collective rituals with the sacred.

On a more functional level, the church provides the new ar-

* Both Catholics and Evangelicals have been particularly militant in recent Central American history. See Golden and McConnell 1986; Bonpane 1985.

rivals with certain networks facilitating the process of settling in the host society. The religious sanctuary movement has given shelter to some families from Central America (see Golden and McConnell 1986). A local Catholic church offered the new arrivals legal advice as well as referral services. Some informants also reported finding jobs, getting temporary loans and babysitting jobs through church connections. Liberation theology, the movement within the Catholic church, particularly strong in Latin America, that in the last decades has preached "the struggle to construct a just and fraternal society, where people can live with dignity and be the agents of their own destiny" (Gutierrez 1973: x), has also affected the new arrivals. Some informants noted that the Catholic church in Central America came under increasing assault by the death squads and the military as it attempted to organize *cursillos* (seminars) to aid peasants and Indians in their demands for basic rights (see Bonpane 1985). And, of course, all Salvadoreans vividly remember the assassination of Archbishop Oscar Arnulfo Romero in March 1980 in San Salvador.

Although Vlach (1984) reports that some of the Guatemalan immigrant families she studied had become somewhat detached from the Catholic church, some of the sermons by the "guerrillas of peace" (Bonpane 1985) may not have been forgotten. As one informant said, *Ante El Señor, somos todos iguales* (Before the Lord, we are all equal).

The continuing key concern running through the lives of the Central American youths was a wish to achieve in order to nurture one's parents and other less fortunate relatives. This specific familistic charity, surely related to a broader concept of religious charity that has flourished through the Central American religious landscape in the past three decades, was rediscovered and intensified as the immigrants settled in the new land. I would argue that this, not independence, is at the heart of the immigrants' motivational dynamics. We have observed the recurrence of an achievement-nurturance cluster in the projective imagery in their TAT narratives, and how the responses to Card 2 of the TAT were almost predictable: the heroine achieves in order to help end parental sacrifice. McClelland's model would have predicted, however, that the heroine would wish to leave her unsuccessful relatives behind, in an Hermesian quest for individualistic self-advancement. The Central American data show quite the opposite pattern.

The family dynamics that fostered a high need achievement among the new arrivals was almost the opposite of McClelland's model of familial aloofness and frigidity. Perceptions of parental sacrifice were a subtle concern to be factored into the motivational dynamics of the youngsters, most of whom were keenly aware of the continuities in a chain of mutual nurturance and affiliation. Rather than viewing their parents as cold and aloof, the new arrivals saw them as warm and caring individuals, who had sacrificed tremendously to settle them in the safety of the United States. The projective data captured the youngsters' perceptions of parental warmth quite movingly. In Card 2 of the TAT the parental figures were regularly pictured as sacrificing so the heroine could attain an education, and thus avoid having to endure the hardships the parents had endured. "They don't want me to live the kind of life they had to endure" was a theme I heard many times from the lips of the new arrivals.

The Central American case presented here does not fit McClelland's model of achievement motivation. The most motivated and successful of the new immigrants from Central America were not individualists seeking self-advancement and independence. Rather, they were motivated by the dream to help others. We have seen how their deeds in the new land strongly suggest this pattern. I have explored how the youngsters work, most commonly to help alleviate parental burdens. As one informant put it in referring to his parents, "Now it is my turn to take care of them." The ethnographic record captured another facet of this achievement-nurturance cluster, in the efforts of the older, more experienced youth to tutor the younger, more recent arrivals and otherwise help them in their first steps in the new land.

New Directions for Research

Based on my analysis of McClelland's model of achievement motivation, I have argued that his achievement-independence association may indeed be an Anglo-American/Northern European oicotype, limited to a given sociocultural climate and therefore less valid in a cross-cultural context (see De Vos 1973:

167–86). There are inherent risks in the misapplication of such models to explain the issues facing other peoples in other places. For example, it has been argued in the case of the Hispanic Americans that some stifling cultural matrix orienting individuals heavily to the family is responsible for crippling achievement motivation, that Hispanic families "hinder mobility" and achievement in school "by stressing . . . family ties, honor, masculinity, values that hinder mobility—and by neglecting values that are conducive to mobility, achievement, independence and deferred gratification" (Heller 1966: 35). Such thinking is often based on an erroneous definition of independence training as a sine qua non for high achievement motivation.

The inescapable image in the narratives is that an overemphasis on family ties and lack of sufficient independence training retard achievement motivation. An article on the school dropout problem among Mexican Americans in Texas suggests that there is "something about the relationship of the Hispanic family to the fact that 45 percent of Hispanic youths never graduate from high school" (La Franchi 1985: 21). More recently a front-page article in the *New York Times* on Hispanic college problems declared, "The reasons that Hispanic-Americans lag behind other groups in college enrollment are diverse, ranging from language barriers and *strong family ties* that discourage Hispanic youths from venturing into the unfamiliar world of higher education to early schooling in ill-funded and overcrowded classrooms and a lack of encouragement from teachers and counselors" (Fiske 1988: 1, 16, my emphasis). The inescapable image is that family traditions of interdependence, cooperation and mutual nurturance somehow impede the growth of achievement motivation and the school success of children; that Hispanic children, not sufficiently trained in independence patterns, remain somehow caught in a family web of counterproductive values (see Carter and Segura 1979: 75–122).

Such reasoning typically leads to variants of an assimilative genre, where cultural diversities are eventually truncated. Richard Rodriguez's tale (1982) is one such version, where achievement was possible only at the expense of turning away from family and community. The price of his achievement was a severe sense of alienation. This need not be the only alternative: the permutations of the human spirit are too varied and too complex to be reduced to single encompassing formulae. In the case of the Central American immigrants, we identified the emergence of a worldview that orients the self to others in the process of resettling in the new land. Recent American immigrants had escaped a world of limited opportunity at best, of death and destruction at the worst, and they entered a radically different socioeconomic reality. In the context of such change, an immigrant ethic emerged wherein it became possible to turn toward one's social group to help and to nurture. New perceptions of opportunity combine with specific family dynamics to motivate students to work hard, to study hard, for a better tomorrow. In the inner-city schools to which the immigrant youngsters have been routed, there are also problems of nonsuccess, explanations of which must take into account the legacy of war, gatekeeping patterns, work demands, the legal barrier, and other hurdles that have to be overcome.

During a year of ethnographic observations, aided by the use of the TAT and by long interviews, I noted the emergence in this particular cohort of Central Americans of a relatively high degree of achievement motivation compared with other samples. But their achievement concerns differed from those reported for the majority of Americans: they were not motivated by any great need for independence, or by a wish for Hermesian self-advancement.

The issues raised in this book suggest some opportunities for further research. I think there is great need for more research among Central American immigrants, a new immigrant group that is largely unknown in the scholarly literature. We need more data on a wide range of variables, from basic demographic issues such as how many Central Americans now make the United States their place of residence, to more long-term studies on economic integration and psychological adjustment. The data upon which this work rests are valid for a specific period of time in the new immigrants' journey: their first experiences in the new land. Not one of my informants had been in the United States for over five years, and many had been here for less than a year. Also, this cohort of immigrants, having escaped a specific social climate, shares certain unique experiences and interpersonal issues, for example, proneness to guilt over selective survival. Clearly, we shall need longitudinal data to capture further changes in their interpersonal concerns and adaptations.

One immediate issue that could conceivably affect the lives of many new arrivals is related to their legal status in the United States. Yet even if the California court decision stands, and colleges and universities can no longer refuse to accept an undocumented candidate, life without the required documentation is greatly complicated. Although the Immigration Reform and Control Act of 1986 offers some amnesty to aliens who can prove they entered the United States and have lived here continuously since 1982, hundreds of thousands of new arrivals from Central America, some in my own sample, have entered the country since then. Deportations of Central Americans could increase greatly. How the new legal marginality of those new arrivals who are able to remain will affect their perceptions of their place in the U.S. opportunity structure is not certain. I doubt that this cohort would remain optimistic about their future in this society if they continue to face immigration problems and other ceilings. Additional data on their changing perceptions of opportunity and on the new strategies that emerge as a consequence of their legal status will be required.

Another issue raised by the data presented here is that, obvious as it may sound, not all Hispanic groups in the United States are alike. When Ronald Reagan, upon returning from a presidential tour of Central and South America in November of 1982, remarked, "You'd be surprised—they are all different countries" down there (Diskin 1983: xv), he articulated an almost studied ignorance in the United States about the distinct realities of the various Hispanic groups. Yet Mexican Americans, Mejicanos, Puerto Rican Americans, Cuban Americans, Americans of South American origin, and the more recent arrivals from Central America are distinct populations, each facing different realities, each with its own subtle set of interpersonal concerns, worldview, and adaptation. If we are to move beyond facile stereotypes, we need to understand more fully the differences among these various subgroups.

This takes us to the wider issue of minority status and adaptation in a plural society. It is becoming increasingly evident that models addressing the problems that face ethnic minorities will be overshadowed by more empirically based approaches to the complexities among distinct minority groups. John Obgu has proposed that we begin to analyze the issues facing different *kinds* of ethnic minorities—the castelike minorities, such as Blacks, American Indians, and Chicanos in the United States— as opposed to the problems facing immigrant minorities. This distinction has overall been useful in ordering the data that emerged from my research among immigrants from Central America. The Central American case may not, however, be best suited to exemplify an immigrant paradigm because many of the recent arrivals lack the required formal documentation for residency in the country.

There is also a need to continue to explore the distinct types of problems facing different kinds of minority groups in specific contexts. In the case of the Hispanic Americans, the evidence suggests that not all subgroups face the same problems. Some of the Central American youth among whom I worked preserved their ethnic identity in the process of achieving success in the Anglo-Saxon idiom, for the very reason that their dreams and deeds were embedded in a sociocultural matrix of family and community cooperation, affiliation, and mutual nurturance.

Appendix

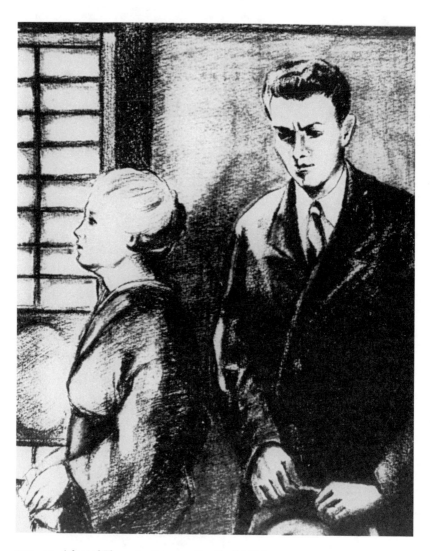

FIG. A1. Adapted Thematic Apperception Card 6 BM

Responses to Selected TAT Cards

The following table summarizes the responses of the Central American immigrants to five of the TAT cards, according to age and sex. Responses to Cards 1, 2, 4, 6BM, 7BM, 8BM, 9BM, and 13B are referred to in the text in varying degrees of detail. Responses to Cards 3BM and 17BM in particular complement our knowledge of basic interpersonal concerns among the new arrivals.

Responses to Card 3BM include a large proportion of narratives about suicide (in 20 percent of the sample), or picture the dramatis persona in a distraught state (in 54 percent of the sample). Loneliness, sadness, and deprivation are some of the basic concerns surfacing in these narratives. These expressions may be isomorphic to the youngster's own sense of loneliness, sadness, and deprivation discussed in detail in Chapters 5, 7, and 8. Responses to Card 17BM include a large proportion of achievement-oriented stories (in 64 percent of the sample). In this case, as in responses to the other cards (notably 1 and 2), the hero is seen as working hard to achieve some future-oriented goal (he becomes a great gymnast and often turns to "help others").

Summary of Central American Immigrants' Responses to TAT Cards,
by Sex and Age

(N = 50)

Theme	Male/Female by Age Group				Percent of Total Responses
	M 14–16 (n = 10)	F 14–16 (n = 10)	M 17–19 (n = 20)	F 17–19 (n = 10)	
Card 3BM					
Suicide	1	3	4	2	20%
Repentance	1	1	4	0	12
Drugs	1	0	2	2	10
Distraught	6	5	10	6	54
Other	1	0	0	0	2
Rejected card	0	1	0	0	2
Card 4					
Couple quarrels	5	3	3	3	28%
Man seeks a fight	2	1	4	2	18
Leaving	0	4	7	1	24
Woman as seductive	2	0	4	1	14
Congenial couple	1	1	1	2	10
Other	0	1	1	0	4
Rejected card	0	1	0	0	2
Card 6BM					
Achievement-Nurturance	2	0	4	1	14%
Mother advises son	0	1	3	2	12
Mother scolds son	2	1	3	2	16
Control	0	1	1	1	6
Leaving	0	0	1	0	2
Return of profligate	3	3	2	2	20
Bad news	2	2	4	2	20
Other	1	1	2	0	8
Rejected card	0	1	0	0	2
Card 7BM					
Mutual cooperation	0	2	5	2	18%
Rebellion	1	0	1	1	6
Status difference/advice	8	4	9	3	48
Other	1	3	5	4	26
Rejected card	0	1	0	0	2
Card 17BM					
Achievement	7	5	13	7	64%
Accident	1	1	2	2	12
Escape	0	1	1	0	4
Illegal behavior	2	0	3	0	10
Descriptive story	0	1	1	1	6
Rejected card	0	2	0	0	4

Reference Matter

References Cited

Adams, Richard N. 1970. *Crucifixion by Power*. Austin, Tex.

Aguayo, Sergio. 1986. "Salvadoreans in Mexico." *Refugees* (New York) 34 (Oct.): 30–31.

Amastae, Jon, and Lucia Elias-Olivares. 1982. *Spanish in the United States: Sociolinguistic Aspects*. New York.

Amnesty International. 1984. *Torture in the Eighties: An Amnesty International Report*. London.

Anderson, Thomas P. 1970. *Matanza*. Lincoln, Nebr.

————. 1982. *Politics in Central America*. New York.

Arroyo, William, and Spencer Eth. 1985. "Children Traumatized by Central American Warfare." In *Post-Traumatic Stress Disorder in Children*, edited by Spencer Eth and Robert S. Pynoos, pp. 103–20. New York.

Baloyra, Enrique. 1982. *El Salvador in Transition*. Chapel Hill, N.C.

Banfield, Edward C. 1958. *The Moral Basis of a Backward Society*. New York.

Barkin, Florence, Elizabeth A. Brandt, and Jacob Ornstein-Galicia. 1982. *Bilingualism and Language Contact: Spanish, English, and Native American Languages*. New York.

Barnouw, Victor. 1979. *Culture and Personality*. Homewood, Ill.

Barry, Tom, and Deb Preusch. 1986. *The Central American Fact Book*. New York.

Bascom, William R. 1965. "Folklore and Anthropology." In *The Study of Folklore*, edited by Alan Dundes, pp. 25–33. Englewood Cliffs, N.J.

Becklund, Laurie. 1985. "Immigrants May Slow Latino Achievement." *Los Angeles Times*, Dec. 10.

Benitez, Mario A., and Lupita G. Villareal. 1979. *The Education of the Mexican American: A Selected Bibliography*. Austin, Tex.

Berry, J. W., and P. R. Dasen, eds. 1974. *Culture and Cognition: Readings on Cross-Cultural Psychology*. London.

Bettelheim, Bruno. 1980. "Surviving." In *Surviving and Other Essays*, by Bruno Bettelheim, pp. 274–314. New York.

Blair, Philip M. 1971. *Job Discrimination and Education: An Investment Analysis.* New York.

—————. 1972. "Job Discrimination and Education." In *Schooling in a Corporate Society: The Political Economy of Education in America,* edited by M. Carnoy, pp. 80–99. New York.

Bloom, Benjamin S., Allison Davis, and Robert Hess. 1965. *Compensatory Education for Cultural Deprivation.* New York.

Bonpane, Blase. 1985. *Guerrillas of Peace: Liberation Theology and the Central American Revolution.* Boston.

Brigham, William T. 1964. *Guatemala, Land of the Quetzal, 1887.* Gainesville, Fla.

Brown, Cynthia, ed. 1985. *With Friends Like These: The Americas Watch Report on Human Rights & U.S. Policy in Latin America.* New York.

Brown, George H., Nan L. Rosen, Susan T. Hill, and Michael Olivas. 1980. *The Condition of Education for Hispanic Americans.* Washington, D.C.: U.S. Department of Education, National Center for Education Statistics.

Buckley, Tom. 1984. *Violent Neighbors: El Salvador, Central America and the United States.* New York.

Cardoso, Fernando H., and Enzo Faletto. 1979. *Dependency and Development in Latin America.* Translated by Marjory Mattingly Urquidi. Berkeley, Calif.

Carter, Thomas P., and R. D. Segura. 1979. *Mexican Americans in School: A Decade of Change.* New York.

Central American Refugee Committee. 1985. *National Bulletin* (San Francisco, Calif.) 1(2): 1–8.

Chavez, John R. 1984. *The Lost Land: The Chicano Image of the Southwest.* Albuquerque, N. Mex.

Chomsky, Noam. 1985. *Turning the Tide: U.S. Intervention in Central America and the Struggle for Peace.* Boston.

Cicourel, Aaron, and John F. Kitsuse. 1963. *The Educational Decision-Makers.* Indianapolis, Ind.

Colson, Elizabeth F. 1974. Foreword to *The Next Generation: An Ethnography of Education in an Urban Neighborhood,* by John U. Ogbu. New York.

Cornelius, Wayne A. 1978. *Mexican Migration to the United States: Causes, Consequences and U.S. Responses.* Cambridge, Mass.

—————. 1981. *Immigration, Mexican Development Policy and the Future of U.S.-Mexican Relations.* La Jolla, Calif.

—————. 1982. *Interviewing Undocumented Immigrants: Methodological Reflections Based on Fieldwork in Mexico and the U.S.* La Jolla, Calif.

Cortes, Carlos. 1985. "The Media Curriculum on Ethnic Minorities: The Development and Reinforcement of Images." Paper read at the University of California Linguistic Minorities Conference, Tahoe City, May 30–June 1.

Cross, Harry E., and James A. Sandos. 1981. *Across the Border: Rural Development in Mexico and Recent Migration to the United States.* Berkeley, Calif.

Cuadernos del Tercer Mundo. 1984. "El Salvador: Una bomba de tiempo." 71: 52–54.

Davis, C., Carl Haub, and JoAnee Willette. 1983. *U.S. Hispanics: Changing the Face of America. Population Bulletin* (Washington, D.C.) 38(3).

Davis, Shelton H. 1983. "State Violence and Agrarian Crisis in Guatemala: The Roots of the Indian-Peasant Rebellion." In *Trouble in Our Backyard,* edited by Martin Diskin, pp. 155–71. New York.

De Vos, George A. 1973. *Socialization for Achievement: Essays on the Cultural Psychology of the Japanese.* Berkeley, Calif.

————. 1978. "Selective Permeability and Reference Group Sanctioning: Psychocultural Continuities in Role Degradation." In *Major Social Issues,* edited by John Milton Yinger, pp. 7–24. New York.

————. 1980. "Ethnic Adaptation and Minority Status." *Journal of Cross-Cultural Psychology* 11: 101–24.

————. 1981. "A System of Codification for Interpersonal Concerns in Thematic or Narrative Material." Unpublished paper. Department of Anthropology, University of California, Berkeley.

————. 1982. "Adaptive Strategies in U.S. Minorities." In *Minority Mental Health,* edited by Enrico E. Jones and Sheldon J. Korchin, pp. 74–112. New York.

————. 1983a. "Achievement Motivation and Intra-Family Attitudes in Immigrant Koreans." *Journal of Psychoanalytic Anthropology* 6(1): 25–71.

————. 1983b. "Ethnic Identity and Minority Status: Some Psychocultural Considerations." In *Identity: Personal and Socio-Cultural,* edited by Anita Jacobson-Widding, pp. 90–113. Uppsala, Sweden.

————. 1984. "Ethnic Persistence and Role Degradation: An Illustration from Japan." Paper read at the American-Soviet Symposium on Contemporary Ethnic Processes in the USA and the USSR, New Orleans, La., Apr. 14–16.

De Vos, George A., and Arthur Hippler. 1969. "Cultural Psychology: Comparative Studies of Human Behavior." In *Handbook of Social Psychology,* edited by G. Lindzey and E. Aronson, 4: 323–417. Reading, Mass.

De Vos, George A., and Marcelo M. Suarez-Orozco. 1986. "Child Development in Japan and the United States: Prospectives of Cross-Cultural Comparisons." In *Child Development and Education in Japan,* edited by Harold Stevenson, Hiroshi Azuma, and Kenji Hakuta, pp. 289–98. New York.

————. 1987. "Sacrifice and the Experience of Power." *Journal of Psychoanalytic Anthropology.* 10: 309–40.

Dickey, Christopher. 1987. *With the Contras: A Report in the Wilds of Nicaragua.* New York.

Didion, Joan. 1983. *Salvador.* New York.

Diskin, Martin. 1983. Introduction to *Trouble in our Backyard,* edited by Martin Diskin. New York.

————. 1985. "Political Repression and Official Terror in El Salvador." Paper read at the 84th Annual Meeting of the American Anthropological Association, Washington, D.C., Dec. 4–8.

Dundes, Alan. 1965. "What is Folklore?" In *The Study of Folklore,* edited by Alan Dundes, pp. 1–3. Englewood Cliffs, N.J.

Durham, William H. 1979. *Scarcity and Survival in Central America: Ecological Origins of the Soccer War.* Stanford, Calif.

Earle, Duncan. 1985. "Militarized Development Among the Highland Maya." Paper read at the 84th Annual Meeting of the American Anthropological Association, Washington, D.C., Dec. 4–8.

Erickson, Fred, and G. Mohatt. 1982. "Organization of Participant Structures in Two Classrooms." In *Doing the Ethnography of Schooling,* edited by George D. Spindler, pp. 136–70. New York.

Erickson, Fred, and J. Shultz. 1981. *The Counselor as Gatekeeper: Social Interaction in Interviews.* New York.

Eysenck, H. J. 1971. *The IQ Argument.* New York.

Fagen, Richard. 1983. "Revolution and Crisis in Nicaragua." In *Trouble in our Backyard,* edited by Martin Diskin, pp. 125–54. New York.

Fernandez, Celestino, and Eduardo Marenco. 1980. *Group Conflict, Education and Mexican Americans: A Discussion Paper.* San Francisco, Calif.

Fishman, Joshua, and Gary D. Keller, eds. 1982. *Bilingual Education for Hispanic Students in the United States.* New York.

Fiske, Edward, 1988. "Colleges Are Seeking to Remedy Lag in Their Hispanic Enrollment." *New York Times,* Mar. 20.

Flinn, John. 1985. "'U.N.' of Illegals at Mexico Border," *San Francisco Examiner,* May 19.

Fordham, Signithia, and John U. Ogbu. 1986. "Black Students' School Success: Coping with the Burden of 'Acting White,'" *Urban Review* 18(3): 176–206.

Foster, George M. 1967. "Peasant Society and the Image of Limited Good." In *Peasant Society: A Reader,* edited by Jack M. Potter, May N. Diaz, and George M. Foster, pp. 300–323. Boston.

Freeman, Derek. 1983. *Margaret Mead and Samoa: The Making and Unmaking of an Anthropological Myth.* Cambridge, Mass.

Gamio, Manuel. 1971. *Mexican Immigration to the United States.* New York.

Gardner, D. 1983. *A Nation at Risk.* New York.

Garretson, O. K. 1928. "A Study of Causes of Retardation Among Mexican Children in a Small Public School System in Arizona." *Journal of Educational Psychology* 19: 31–40.

Garth, T. R., and H. D. Johnson. 1934. "The Intelligence and Achievement of Mexican Children in the U.S." *Journal of Abnormal and Social Psychology* 29: 222–39.

Geertz, Clifford. 1973. *The Interpretation of Cultures.* New York.

Gibson, Margaret A. 1983. *Home-School-Community Linkages: A Study of Educational Equity for Punjabi Youths. Final Report.* Washington, D.C.

———. 1987. "Punjabi Immigrants in an American High School." In *Interpretive Ethnography of Education at Home and Abroad,* edited by George D. Spindler and Louise S. Spindler, pp. 281–310. Hillsdale, N.J.

———. In press. *Accommodation Without Assimilation: Punjabi Sikh Immigrants in an American High School and Community.* Ithaca, N.Y.

Goho, Tom, and David Smith. 1973. *A College Degree: Does it Substantially Enhance the Economic Achievement of Chicanos?* Center for Business Services Occasional Paper no. 503, New Mexico State University, Las Cruces.

Golden, Renny, and Michael McConnell. 1986. *Sanctuary: The New Underground Railroad.* New York.

Gottfried, Nathan W. 1973. "Effects of Early Intervention Programs." In *Comparative Studies of Blacks and Whites,* edited by K. S. Miller and R. M. Dreger, pp. 273–93. New York.

Gould, Stephen Jay. 1981. *The Mismeasure of Man.* New York.

Gumperz, John J. 1981. "Conversational Inferences and Classroom Learning." In *Ethnography and Language in Educational Settings,* edited by J. L. Green and C. Wallat, pp. 3–23. Norwood, N.J.

———. 1982. *Language and Social Identity.* London.

———. 1983. "The Communicative Bases of Social Inequality." In *Minorities: Communities and Identity,* edited by C. Fried, pp. 109–18. Berlin.

Gutiérrez, Gustavo. 1973. *A Theology of Liberation: History, Politics and Salvation.* Translated and edited by Sister Caridad Inda and John Eagleson. New York.

Hansen, Donald A. 1986. "Family-School Articulations: The Effects of Interaction Rule Mismatch." *American Educational Research Journal* 23: 643–59.

Hansen, Donald A., and Victoria A. Johnson. 1985. *Classroom Learning Strategies and Orientations Toward Work.* Berkeley, Calif.

Heller, Celia. 1966. *Mexican-American Youth: Forgotten Youth at the Crossroads.* New York.

Henry, William E. 1956. *The Analysis of Fantasy: The Thematic Apperception Technique in the Study of Personality.* New York.

Hispanic Policy Development Project. 1984. *"Make Something Happen": Hispanics and Urban High School Reform*. 2 vols. New York.

Hymes, Dell. 1974. *Foundations in Sociolinguistics*. Philadelphia.

Inbar, Michael. 1976. *The Vulnerable Age Phenomenon*. New York.

Jensen, Arthur R. 1969. "How Much Can We Boost I.Q. and Scholastic Achievement?" *Harvard Educational Review*, reprint series 2: 1–123.

Johnson, Kenneth R. 1970. *Teaching the Culturally Disadvantaged: A Rational Approach*. Palo Alto, Calif.

Jones, Ernest. 1925. "Mother-Right and the Sexual Ignorance of Savages." *International Journal of Psychoanalysis* 6: 109–30.

Joseph, Gilbert, and Allen Wells. 1985. "Political Terror in Nicaragua: The 'Contra' War." Paper read at the 84th Annual Meeting of the American Anthropological Association, Washington, D.C., Dec. 4–8.

Kempton, Murray. 1986. "Scenes from Nicaragua." *New York Review of Books* 33(13): 5–11.

Kesser, Thomas, and Betty B. Caroli. 1982. *Today's Immigrants: Their Stories*. New York.

Killian, L. R. 1971. "WISC, Illinois Test of Psycholinguistic Abilities, and Bender Visual-Motor Gestalt Test Performance of Spanish-American Kindergarten and First-Grade School Children." *Journal of Consulting and Clinical Psychology* 37: 38–43.

Kim, Kwan S., and David F. Ruccio, eds. 1985. *Debt and Development in Latin America*. Notre Dame, Ind.

Knowlton, Clark S. 1979. "Some Demographic, Economic, and Educational Considerations on Mexican American Youth." Paper read at the Southwestern Sociological Association Meeting, Fort Worth, Tex.

LaFeber, Walter. 1984. *Inevitable Revolutions: The United States in Central America*. New York.

LaFranchi, Howard. 1985. "Hispanic Family Ties Are Cause and Cure of Hispanic Dropout Dilemma." *Christian Science Monitor*, Apr. 22.

Lancaster, Clarise, and Frederick J. Scheuren. 1977. "Counting the Uncountable Illegals: Some Initial Statistical Speculations Employing Capture-Recapture Techniques." Paper read at the Annual Meeting of the American Statistical Association, Washington, D.C.

Lefkowitz, Bernard. 1985. "Renegotiating Society's Contract with Public Schools: The National Commission on Secondary Education for Hispanics and the National Board of Inquiry into Schools." *Carnegie Quarterly* 29(4): 2–11.

Leiken, Robert S. 1986. "The Battle for Nicaragua." *New York Review of Books* 33(4): 43–52.

LeVine, Robert A. 1967. *Dreams and Deeds: Achievement Motivation in Nigeria*. Chicago.

Lewis, Sasha G. 1980. *Slave Trade Today: American Exploitation of Illegal Aliens.* Boston.

Lieberson, Stanley. 1980. *A Piece of the Pie: Black and White Immigrants Since 1880.* Berkeley, Calif.

Lindzey, Gardner. 1961. *Projective Techniques and Cross-Cultural Research.* New York.

Lopez y Rivas, Gilberto. 1973. *The Chicanos: Life and Struggles of the Mexican Minority in the United States.* Translated by Elizabeth Martinez and Gilberto Lopez y Rivas. New York.

Lowie, Robert H. 1937. *The History of Ethnological Theory.* New York.

McClelland, David C. 1961. *The Achieving Society.* Princeton, N.J.

————. 1984. *Motives, Personality and Society: Selected Papers.* New York.

McClelland, David C., ed. 1955. *Studies in Motivation.* New York.

McClelland, David C., J. W. Atkinson, R. A. Clark, and E. L. Lowell. 1953. *The Achievement Motive.* New York.

McClelland, David C., A. L. Baldwin, U. Bronfenbrenner, and F. L. Strodtbeck. 1958. *Talent and Society: New Perspectives in the Identification of Talent.* Princeton, N.J.

McColm, R. Bruce. 1982. *El Salvador, Peaceful Revolution or Armed Struggle?* New York.

McDermott, R. P. 1974. "Achieving School Failure: An Anthropological Approach to Illiteracy and Social Stratification." In *Education and Cultural Processes: Toward an Anthropology of Education*, edited by George D. Spindler, pp. 82–117. New York.

McWilliams, Carey. 1968. *North from Mexico: The Spanish-Speaking People of the United States.* New York.

Maestas, Leo C. 1981. "Ethnicity and High School Student Achievement Across Rural and Urban Districts." *Educational Research Quarterly* 6: 32–42.

Malinowski, Bronislaw. 1927. *Sex and Repression in Savage Society.* London.

————. 1929. *The Sexual Life of Savages.* New York.

Matute-Bianchi, Maria Eugenia. 1985. "Chicanos and the Oppositional Process: The Historical Creation of a Collective Identity." Paper read at the University of California Linguistic Minorities Conference, Tahoe City, May 30–June 1.

Mead, Margaret. 1928. *Coming of Age in Samoa.* New York.

Mehan, H. 1978. "Structuring School Structure." *Harvard Educational Review* 45(1): 311–38.

Mohn, Sid L. 1983. *Central American Refugees: The Search for Appropriate Responses.* World Refugee Survey, 25th anniversary issue: 42–47.

Monge, W., R. Baca, and B. Dexter. 1977. *Undocumented Workers: Illegal*

Immigration and Exclusionary Status Among the Spanish Surnamed in Los Angeles. Dominguez Hills, Calif.

Montagu, Ashley, ed. 1975. *Race and IQ.* London.

Montgomery, Tommie Sue. 1982. *Revolution in El Salvador: Origins and Evolution.* Boulder, Colo.

Murray, Henry A. 1943. *Thematic Apperception Test Manual.* Cambridge, Mass.

———. 1951. "Toward a Classification of Interactions." In *Toward a General Theory of Action,* edited by T. Parsons and E. Shils, pp. 434–65. Cambridge, Mass.

Nash, Manning. 1967. *Machine Age Maya: The Industrialization of a Guatemalan Community.* Chicago.

Neier, Aryeh. 1986. "The US and the Contras." *New York Review of Books* 33(6): 3–6.

Ogbu, John U. 1974. *The Next Generation: An Ethnography of Education in an Urban Neighborhood.* New York.

———. 1978. *Minority Education and Caste: The American System in Cross-Cultural Perspective.* New York.

———. 1981. "Origins of Human Competence: A Cultural-Ecological Perspective." *Child Development* 52: 413–29.

———. 1982a. "Anthropology and Education." In *International Encyclopedia of Education: Research and Studies.* pp. 276–98. Oxford.

———. 1982b. "Minority Status and Schooling in Plural Societies." Unpublished paper. Department of Anthropology, University of California, Berkeley.

———. 1983. "Indigenous and Immigrant Minority Education: A Comparative Perspective." Paper read at 82nd Annual Meeting of the American Anthropological Association, Chicago, Nov. 16–20.

———. 1984. "Knowledge, Identity and Minority Education in Plural Societies." Paper read at the First International Jerusalem Convention on Education, Jerusalem, Israel, Dec. 19–23.

———. 1985. "Variability in Minority School Performance: A Problem in Search of an Explanation." Paper read at the University of North Carolina, Raleigh, Apr. 12.

Ogbu, John U., and Maria Eugenia Matute-Bianchi. 1986. "Understanding Sociocultural Factors: Knowledge, Identity, and School Adjustment." In *Beyond Language: Social & Cultural Factors in Schooling Language Minority Students,* pp. 73–142. Sacramento, Calif.

Pear, Robert. 1987. "Duarte Appeals to Reagan to Let Salvadoreans Stay." *New York Times,* Apr. 26.

Perera, Victor. 1986. "Can Guatemala Change?" *New York Review of Books* 33(13): 39–43.

Piaget, Jean. 1930. *The Child's Conception of Physical Causality.* London.

Piaget, Jean, and Barbel Inhelder. 1969. *The Psychology of the Child*. New York.

Piore, Michael J. 1979. *Birds of Passage: Migrant Labor and Industrial Societies*. New York.

Portes, Alejandro. 1978. "Towards a Structural Analysis of Illegal (Undocumented) Immigration." *International Migration Review* 44: 469–84.

Portes, Alejandro, and Robert L. Bach. 1985. *Latin Journey. Cuban and Mexican Immigrants in the United States*. Berkeley, Calif.

Quezada, Sergio Aguayo. 1985. "Exodo centroamericano." *NEXOS* 3: 37–42.

Quiroz, Roman M. 1982. Introduction to *Revolution in El Salvador*, by Tommie Sue Montgomery. Boulder, Colo.

Raskin, Leslie, 1987. "Changing Kibbutzniks' Attitudes." Paper read at the Institute of Personality Assessment and Research, University of California, Berkeley, Sept. 21.

Riding, Alan. 1984. *Distant Neighbors: A Portrait of the Mexicans*. New York.

Riessman, Frank. 1962. *The Culturally Deprived Child*. New York.

Rodriguez, Richard. 1982. *Hunger of Memory: The Education of Richard Rodriguez. An Autobiography*. Boston.

Romo, Harriet. 1984. "The Mexican Origin Population's Differing Perceptions of Their Children's Schooling." *Social Science Quarterly* 65: 635–49.

Rosen, Bernard C., and R. D'Andrade. 1965. "The Psychosocial Origins of Achievement Motivation." In *Readings in Child Development and Personality*, edited by Paul H. Mussen, J. J. Conger, and J. Kagan, pp. 375–99. New York.

Rosenbaum, Robert J. 1981. *Mexicano Resistance in the Southwest: "The Sacred Right of Self-Preservation."* Austin, Tex.

Rosenblatt, Roger. 1984. *Children of War*. New York.

Samora, Julian. 1971. *Los Mojados: The Wetback Story*. Notre Dame, Ind.

Scarry, Elaine. 1985. *The Body in Plain: The Making and Unmaking of the World*. Oxford.

Scheper-Hughes, Nancy. 1979. *Saints, Scholars and Schizophrenics: Mental Illness in Rural Ireland*. Berkeley, Calif.

———. 1985. "Culture, Scarcity, and Maternal Thinking: Maternal Detachment and Infant Survival in a Brazilian Shantytown." *Ethos* 13(4): 291–317.

Segesvary, Louis S. 1984. *Guatemala: A Complex Scenario*. Vol. 6, no. 3, Significant Issues Series, Center for Strategic Studies, Georgetown University.

Sheehan, Edward R. F. 1986. "The 'Clean' War." *New York Review of Books* 33(11): 25–30.

Shostak, Marjorie. 1983. *Nisa: The Life and Words of a !Kung Woman*. New York.

Spence, Janet T. 1983. *Achievement and Achievement Motives: Psychological and Sociological Approaches*. San Francisco, Calif.

Spiro, Melford E. 1954. "Human Nature in Its Psychological Dimensions." *American Anthropologist* 56: 19–30.

———. 1982. *Oedipus in the Trobriands*. Chicago.

Stewart, Abigail J., ed. 1982. *Motivation and Society: A Volume in Honor of David C. McClelland*. San Francisco, Calif.

Suarez-Orozco, Marcelo M. 1986. "Spaanse Amerikanen: Vergelijkende Beschouwingen en Onderwijsproblemen. Tweede Generatie Immigrantenjogeren." *Cultuur en Migratie* (Brussels) 2: 21–49.

———. 1987a. "Towards a Psycho-Social Understanding of Hispanic Adaptation to American Schooling." In *Success or Failure? Learning and the Language Minority Student*, edited by Henry T. Trueba, pp. 156–68. Cambridge, Mass.

———. 1987b. "Transformations in Perception of Self and Social Environment in Mexican Immigrants." In *People in Upheaval*, edited by Scott Morgan and Elizabeth F. Colson, pp. 129–43. Staten Island, N.Y.

———. 1987c. "Hispanic Americans: Comparative Considerations and the Educational Problems of Children." *International Migration* (Geneva) 25(2): 141–64.

———. 1987d. "Treatment of Children in the 'Dirty War': Ideology, State Terrorism and the Abuse of Children in Argentina." In *Child Survival*, edited by Nancy Scheper-Hughes, pp. 227–46. Dordrecht, Netherlands.

Taussig, Michael. 1987. *Shamanism, Colonialism, and the Wild Man: A Study in Terror and Healing*. Chicago.

Timerman, Jacobo. 1981. *Prisoner Without a Name, Cell Without a Number*. New York.

Torres-Rivas, Edelberto. 1983. "Central America Today: A Study in Regional Dependency." In *Trouble in Our Backyard*, edited by Martin Diskin, pp. 1–33. New York.

Trueba, Henry T. 1987. "Introduction: The Ethnography of Schooling." In *Success or Failure? Learning and the Language Minority Student*, edited by Henry T. Trueba, pp. 1–13. Cambridge, Mass.

Tylor, Paul S. 1976. *Mexican Migration to the United States*. New York.

U.S. Department of State. 1984. *Guatemala: Background Notes*. Washington, D.C.

———. 1985. *El Salvador: Background Notes*. Washington, D.C.

U.S. Immigration and Naturalization Service. 1984. *Statistical Yearbook*. Washington, D.C.

Urrabazo, Rosendo. 1985. "Machismo: Mexican American Male Self-Concept. An Interpretation and Reflection on Thematic Appercep-tion Test and Kinetic Family Drawing Results of Mexican American Teen Agers." Unpublished Ph.D. dissertation, Graduate Theological Union, Berkeley, Calif.

Van Praag, Nicholas. 1986. "Guatemalan Refugees in Chiapas." *Refugees* (New York) 34 (Oct.): 20–22.

Vlach, Norita S. Jones. 1984. "America y el Alma: A Study of Families and Adolescents Who Are Recent United States Immigrants from Guatemala." Unpublished Ph.D. dissertation, Department of Medical Anthropology, University of California, San Francisco.

Wagatsuma, Hiroshi, and George A. De Vos. 1984. *Heritage of Endurance: Family Patterns and Delinquency Formation in Urban Japan.* Berkeley, Calif.

Walker, Constance L. 1987. "Hispanic Achievement: Old Views and New Perspectives." In *Success or Failure? Learning and the Language Minority Student,* edited by Henry T. Trueba, pp. 15–32. Cambridge, Mass.

Weber, David J., ed. 1973. *Foreigners in Their Native Lands: Historical Roots of the Mexican Americans.* Albuquerque, N. Mex.

Weber, Max. 1958. *The Protestant Ethic and the Spirit of Capitalism.* Translated by Talcott Parsons. New York.

West, Robert C., and John P. Augelli. 1976. *Middle America: Its Lands and Peoples,* 2d ed. Englewood Cliffs, N.J.

Wolf, Eric R. 1969. *Peasant Wars of the Twentieth Century.* New York.

Womack, John, Jr. 1983. Foreword to *Trouble in Our Backyard,* edited by Martin Diskin. New York.

Zintz, Miles. 1963. *Education Across Cultures.* Dubuque, Iowa.

Index

In this index an "f" after a number indicates a separate reference on the next page, and an "ff" indicates separate references on the next two pages. A continuous discussion over two or more pages is indicated by a span of page numbers, e.g., "57–59." *Passim* is used for a cluster of references in close but not consecutive sequence.

Library of Congress Cataloging-in-Publication Data

Suarez-Orozco, Marcelo M., 1956–
    Central American refugees and U.S. high schools : a psychosocial study of motivation and achievement / Marcelo M. Suarez-Orozco.
        p.   cm.
    Bibliography: p.
    Includes index.
    ISBN 0-8047-1498-3 (alk. paper)
    1. Latin Americans—Education (Secondary)—United States.   2. Refugees—United States.   3. Refugees— Central America.   4. Latin American students—United States—Attitudes.   5. Academic achievement. I. Title.   II. Title: Central American refugees and U.S. high schools.
LC2670.4.S82   1989
373.18'08968073—dc19   88-29315
                                                              CIP